STRATEGY@WORK

From Design To Delivery

A Brightline and Thinkers50 collaboration bringing together the very best thinking and insights in the field of strategy and beyond

www.brightline.org
www.thinkers50.com

Introduction

If you ask a manager what excites them about their job, what gets them out of bed in the morning, what provides meaning to their work, their answers tend to be similar no matter where they are in the world, who they work for or what their job is.

Distilled to three words it is: Getting things done.

It doesn't matter if they're running a production line in Qingdao, managing a team in a Silicon Valley giant or overseeing the building of a bridge in Mumbai, managers revel in the sense of completion, of turning a plan or an idea into reality; creating something; implementation. They are only human.

Given this aspiration to get things done, managers and leaders have to deal with a fair amount of frustration along the way. Organizations have a patchy and somewhat indifferent record in transforming ideas, initiatives, strategies and dreams into reality.

Research by Brightline with the Economist Intelligence Unit in 2017 surveyed 500 executives. We found that only one in ten reached their strategic goals, and 53 per cent agreed that poor delivery capability is a source of competitive disadvantage. A total of 59 per cent of survey respondents said that their organizations "often struggle to bridge the gap between strategy development and its practice, day-to-day implementation".

"The reason strategy execution is often glossed over by even the most astute strategy consultants is because it's not a strategy challenge. It's a human behaviour one," argues Peter Bregman in a recent *Harvard Business Review* article. "To deliver stellar results, people need to be hyper-aligned and laser-focused on the highest-impact actions that will drive the organization's most important outcomes. But even in well-run, stable organizations, people are misaligned, too broadly focused and working at cross-purposes."

Getting things done is hard and difficult work. We live in turbulent times and creating robust and effective business strategies is hugely demanding. Turning them into reality equally so.

The Brightline Initiative aims to help organizations and managers to make sense of these challenges and to make better decisions as they create and implement strategies. It is a coalition dedicated to helping organizations bridge the gap between strategy design and strategy delivery.

Working with our partners at Thinkers50 we have created *Strategy@Work*. It showcases some of the very best thinkers in the field of strategy and beyond. We hope that it acts as a catalyst for readers to get things done.

Ricardo Viana Vargas
Executive Director
The Brightline Initiative

www.brightline.org

Resources
Economist Intelligence Unit and the Project Management Institute, "Why Good Strategies Fail", 2013

Peter Bregman, "Execution is a People Problem, Not a Strategy Problem", *Harvard Business Review*, January 4 2017

Contents

Acknowledgements

Strategy execution is always a team effort and *Strategy@Work* is no exception. From the Brightline Inititiative, Ricardo Vargas, Edivandro Conforto and Tahirou Assane moved between the big picture and the nitty gritty of detail.

Viki Jebens of Jebens Design provided her usual reassurance and design excellence in guiding the manuscript from a pile of paper to a finished book.

And, we would like to thank all of the thinkers and practitioners who were kind enough to lend us their time and ideas.

Stuart Crainer & Des Dearlove
Thinkers50

www.thinkers50.com

'AN OUNCE OF ACTION IS WORTH A TON OF THEORY.'

FRIEDRICH ENGELS

Essential Thinkers

The Brightline Initiative Thinkers50 Strategy Award for 2017 shortlisted eight key thinkers changing our understanding of strategy and how it is put to work:

1. Weiru Chen

Weiru Chen is an associate professor of strategy at the China Europe International Business School, where he teaches industry and competitive analysis, business model innovation, and strategy. He is the author (with Cho-Hsuan Yu) of *Platform Strategy: Business Model Revolution*, a Chinese bestseller based on a study of 40 Chinese firms and 20 global companies.

2. Richard D'Aveni

The Bakala Professor of Strategy at the Tuck School of Business at Dartmouth College, D'Aveni is the author of a number of influential books including *Hypercompetition* (Free Press, 1994), *Beating the Commodity Trap* (HBR Press, 2009) and *Strategic Capitalism* (McGraw-Hill, 2012). His forthcoming book, *When Titans Rule the World* (Houghton Mifflin Harcourt, 2018), builds on his HBR article "3-D Printing Will Change the World," and charts the rise of "panindustrial" manufacturers.

3. Pankaj Ghemawat

Indian-born Pankaj Ghemawat is the professor of management and strategy and director of the Center for the Globalization of Education and Management at the Stern School of Business. He is also the Anselmo Rubiralta Professor of Global Strategy at IESE Business School in Spain. He is the author of *World 3.0: Global Prosperity and How to Achieve it* (HBR Press, 2011) and *The Laws of Globalization* (Cambridge, 2017).

4. W Chan Kim & Renée Mauborgne

The authors of the bestseller *Blue Ocean Strategy* (HBR, 2005), which has sold more than 3.5 million copies, Kim and Mauborgne are professors of strategy at INSEAD and co-directors of the INSEAD *Blue Ocean Strategy* Institute. Most recently, they are the authors of *Blue Ocean Shift* (Hachette, 2017).

5. Rita G McGrath

On the faculty of Columbia Business School since 1993, Rita McGrath is the author of *The End of Competitive Advantage* (Harvard, 2013). She is also co-author of *MarketBusters: 40 Strategic Moves that Drive Exceptional Business Growth* (HBR Press, 2005) and *The Entrepreneurial Mindset* (HBR Press, 2000). Her next project, tentatively entitled "Discovery Driven Advantage" examines how companies can build true proficiency in innovation.

6. Roger Martin

The former dean of the Rotman School of Management at the University of Toronto, Martin is the Institute Director of the Martin Prosperity Institute at Rotman where he holds the Premier's Chair in Productivity and Competitiveness. He is the author of nine books including *Getting Beyond Better* (with Sally Osberg, HBR Press, 2015), *Playing to Win* (with AG Lafley, HBR Press, 2013) and *Creating Great Choices* (with Jennifer Riel, HBR Press, 2017). He is a two-time Thinkers50 Award winner.

7. Alex Osterwalder & Yves Pigneur

Yves Pigneur is a Belgian computer scientist and Alex Osterwalder is a Swiss consultant, and founder of Strategyzer. They are the authors of *Business Model Generation* (Wiley, 2010), which has sold more than one million copies in 30 languages. They invented the "Business Model Canvas," used by companies worldwide. The original book has been followed by *Business Model You* (Wiley, 2012) and *Value Proposition Design* (Wiley, 2014).

8. András Tilcsik

Hungarian-born Tilcsik is an assistant professor of strategic management at the Rotman School of Management and a faculty fellow at the Michael Lee-Chin Family Institute for Corporate Citizenship. In 2015, he and Chris Clearfield won the Bracken Bower Prize from McKinsey and the *Financial Times*, given to the best business book proposal by scholars under 35. The book, *Meltdown: Why Our Systems Fail and What We Can Do About It* is forthcoming (Penguin, 2018).

MARK A. LANGLEY

Bridging the gap between strategy design and implementation

Ninety percent of executives in a recent research study admitted they failed to implement some part of their strategy successfully. That wastes money, destroys productivity and it is bad for morale.

Put another way, every 20 seconds, one million dollars is wasted due to poor organization performance. That's two trillion dollars every year – equivalent to the GDP of Brazil – and it's too much.

Perhaps this is because having the idea, designing a strategy, or dreaming a dream is easy. Delivering the strategy, implementing change, and making the dream come true is much harder and tends to get left behind by senior executives who move on to the next big idea before the last one takes hold.

All strategic change in organizations happens through projects and programmes – it simply cannot happen any other way. Think about this: how could a company become a digital enterprise without a software upgrade project, or a dozen of them? How would an organization enter new markets if it doesn't have a programme that integrates its newest acquisition? How could a business unit optimize its product portfolio without a series of projects designed to retire its poor performers?

According to research done by the Economist Intelligence Unit in collaboration with the Project Management Institute (PMI), 88 per cent of executives say that successful execution of their strategic initiatives will be "essential" or "very important" to their organizations' competitiveness in the next few years. About two-thirds say they struggle with day-to-day implementation of strategy and more than half say this weakness in delivering their strategy puts them at a competitive disadvantage.

Leading organizations do three things better than their peers:

1. insist on visible and consistent executive-level commitment to building implementation muscle;

2. motivate cross-functional collaboration between strategy designers and deliverers

3. master a full array of delivery capabilities that are deployed in a flexible framework

For most organizations, the solution already exists in the form of its delivery capability – whatever it is called: transformation office, results delivery authority, or simply project or programme management.

PMI and the professionals we represent care about that delivery capability. We know that when executives care about it too, their organizations are more successful and they waste less money – 28 times less than their counterparts who don't draw a bright line between strategy design and delivery.

And that's what is possible when effective, energetic execution complements first-class strategy design.

About the author

 Mark A. Langley is the President and Chief Executive Officer of the Project Management Institute.

'DO WHAT'S RIGHT. DO IT RIGHT. DO IT RIGHT NOW.'

BC FORBES

PERRY KEENAN, JEANNE KWONG BICKFORD,
PETER TOLLMAN, AND GRANT FREELAND

The hard truth of change

No-one reading this article will need any convincing that many businesses today are operating in an environment of rapid, possibly unprecedented, change. The stakes are high. Depending on complexity, 50 to 75 per cent of change efforts fail. And these days, the bulk of the change being undertaken is at the complex end of the spectrum, with the straightforward things having long since been done.

Framing and quantifying this dynamic, the business world, like the geopolitical world, has entered a new age of uncertainty. Turbulence is affecting more sectors, more frequently, and more severely. One-time market leaders or corporate giants can fall rapidly from grace, having failed to adjust to new realities, or losing out to more nimble competitors. Blackberry and Blockbuster are among the high-profile casualties. In fact, companies are expiring more quickly than ever before: the expectation is that one third of all public companies will disappear within the next five years. For a striking impression of the landscape, see the sidebar, "Most sectors are experiencing volatility unmatched in decades."

Adapt or perish

Most of the drivers of today's fast-paced business environment are well recognized – economic turbulence, disruptive technology, globalization, and fierce competition being the main culprits. The imperative for many businesses is to adapt to the changing conditions in order to boost their company's performance. Traditional sources of competitive advantage, like scale and proprietary assets, are less valuable and less sustainable in this volatile environment.

To this unpredictable mix can be added digital transformation, advanced data analytics, robotics, artificial intelligence, and more agile methods of cooperation and delivery. Potentially, these forces have the power to make the way we will work in 10-20 years from now almost unrecognizable to today's business leaders.

Collectively, these dynamics will create both great challenges and great opportunities. Paraphrasing Darwin, it is not the strongest of the species that survives, but the most adaptable.

Most sectors are experiencing volatility unmatched in decades

Since the start of the S&P 500, company fortunes have become far less stable across industries and geographies, particularly since the early 1990s. Exhibit 1 shows the volatility of all US public companies, via their annual changes in market capitalization. The light shading represents periods of stable company value; the dark shading represents periods of widely fluctuating company value. Note how even historically calm sectors, such as energy and telecom, have been experiencing high volatility in the last decade or two.

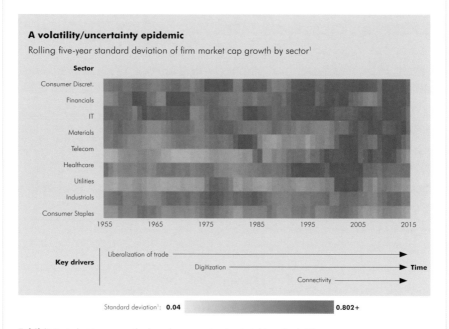

Exhibit 1: Industries across the board are experiencing heightened volatility

1. Average five-year rolling standard deviation of % firm market cap growth by sector, weighted by firm market cap
2. 95th percentile of standard deviation across sectors. Note: Based on all public U.S. companies

We could talk a lot about the common fatal flaws in big change efforts, the criticality of vision, leadership alignment and activation, activist governance, stakeholder engagement, "always on transformation", and so forth. However, for the purpose of brevity, we will restrict ourselves to two points.

First, the bulk of adaptation to the new fast-paced environment will rely on an organization's people significantly changing their behaviours and actions, to take on new roles, to cooperate with their peers in very different ways, to move at pace and with often uncomfortable uncertainty, to make tough decisions and to support their friends and colleagues who struggle with the transition. An absolute premium will need to be placed on thinking through the people considerations in conjunction with whatever exciting technological or data capabilities may arise.

Yet, comparatively little has been written on the specifics of the people-related components of the changes ahead. This is all the more surprising given that there are fundamental forces on both the supply and demand side dynamics for people and talent that are likely to further fuel the dramatic pace of business change.

Second, much of the upcoming changes that organizations will face will be launched and landed though strategic programmes and initiatives. The ability of organizations to adapt and survive hinges on the delivery of these programmes and their component initiatives. Therefore, a premium will exist for having the right capabilities to ensure their success.

People AND technology

Our BCG colleagues Vikram Bhalla, Susanne Drychs, and Rainer Strack have led an extensive effort examining global megatrends and how they will impact both the demand for, and supply of, talent. They have grouped these megatrends into 12 primary forces. These forces are summarized in terms of their impact on the supply and demand for talent in exhibits two and three, overleaf.

Together these forces will revolutionize the way that work gets done in companies and will compel leaders to rethink even the most basic assumptions about how their organizations function. They will need to discover new ways of organizing, performing, and leading, along with new approaches to recruiting, developing, and engaging employees – all this in organizations with limitless data, open boundaries, employees and machines working side-by-side, and with a rapidly evolving employee value proposition.

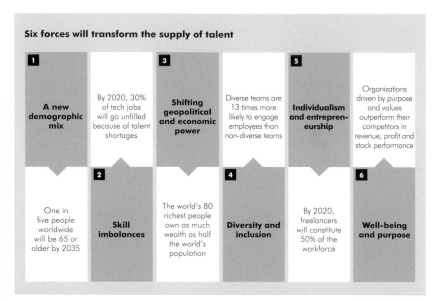

Six forces will transform the supply of talent

1 A new demographic mix

By 2020, 30% of tech jobs will go unfilled because of talent shortages

3 Shifting geopolitical and economic power

Diverse teams are 13 times more likely to engage employees than non-diverse teams

5 Individualism and entrepreneurship

Organizations driven by purpose and values outperform their competitors in revenue, profit and stock performance

One in five people worldwide will be 65 or older by 2035

2 Skill imbalances

The world's 80 richest people own as much wealth as half the world's population

4 Diversity and inclusion

By 2020, freelancers will constitute 50% of the workforce

6 Well-being and purpose

Exhibit 2: Technology and digital productivity coupled with shifts in ways of generating business value will profoundly affect the supply of talent

Sources: United Nations Population Division, IDG, Oxfam, American Express Open Network, Forbes, BrightHouse

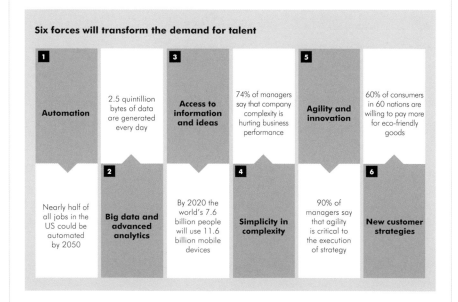

Six forces will transform the demand for talent

1 Automation

2.5 quintillion bytes of data are generated every day

3 Access to information and ideas

74% of managers say that company complexity is hurting business performance

5 Agility and innovation

60% of consumers in 60 nations are willing to pay more for eco-friendly goods

Nearly half of all jobs in the US could be automated by 2050

2 Big data and advanced analytics

By 2020 the world's 7.6 billion people will use 11.6 billion mobile devices

4 Simplicity in complexity

90% of managers say that agility is critical to the execution of strategy

6 New customer strategies

Exhibit 3: Shifts in resource distribution combined with changing workforce culture and values will profoundly impact the demand for talent

Exactly how these forces will manifest themselves will vary depending on the industry and the competitive context. Nevertheless, there will likely be some common threads to the opportunities and challenges to be managed.

- **"Speed and agility necessitates failing fast and learning fast":** Insight into customer needs and competitor moves, combined with the speed and agility to capitalize on this knowledge, will be increasingly critical. Agile development models will become far more common and extend far more broadly into the organization. However, Agile needs to be more than having the product development function organized in scrums, developing user stories, executing in short iterations, using daily stand-ups and working the backlog. Easier said than done, the key to developing Agile as a component of competitive advantage is in actively investing in people and skills development to shape mature business teams with end-to-end representation, securing capable and committed product ownership from the business, developing new models of delivery and openly calling out failures, frequently challenging whether the minimum sufficient conditions for success are in place and effectively orchestrating benefits delivery and issues resolution across the teams. Delighting customers in ways that most impact business success and competitive agility are the goals. Establishing the model of experimenting, learning, adjusting, innovating and, at times failing fast will be essential to building capability and underpinning ongoing success.

- **"What's mine might also be yours":** Organizational boundaries will increasingly blur – not just boundaries within, but also across, organizations. Traditional distinctions and frictions between employees, contractors, suppliers, customers, and, in some considerations, competitors will need to erode. Multidisciplinary teams, the use of contractors and industry learning platforms, and potentially the leverage of crowd sourcing and the sharing economy will all become increasing features in how work is done. As these new ways of working take hold, challenges will need to be tackled in terms of "What is the role of the organization?". The nexus will likely be in balancing between fostering these ecosystems, building connectivity and energizing people for success, while also ensuring the necessary focus on the reinforcement of accountability for outcomes and the creation of economic value.

- **"Manage complexity with smart simplicity":** Increasing competitive intensity, consequent requirements for enhanced innovation and responsiveness, increasing stakeholder engagement across non traditional boundaries and greater regulation all contribute to a substantially increased level of complexity. Today's organizational design constructs are not able to cope with this new level of complexity; they result in complicated, bureaucratic structures and processes. Performance and employee engagement are inevitable casualties. "Smart simplicity" is a new approach developed by BCG, under the leadership of our colleague Yves Morieux, that offers a superior approach to managing this complexity. Rather than adding organizational elements (structures, processes, incentives) in an effort to control what people do, smart simplicity guides leaders to create a context that promotes individual autonomy and alignment of the perceived individual interests of the employees with the interests of the company as a whole. Smart simplicity combines organizational elements in a minimally sufficient way so that it make sense for the employees to cooperate as a team.

Specifically, the approach involves empowering people sufficiently for the requirements of their jobs by giving them the right resources and removing unnecessary constraints, and aligning interests by consequences to actions and results. (For full information on smart simplicity please refer to Yves Morieux and Peter Tollman, *Six Simple Rules – How to Manage Complexity without Getting Complicated*, Harvard Business Review Press, 2014.)

- **"Talent, talent, talent":** The stereotypical mantra of the change management industry has traditionally been "Communicate, communicate, communicate". Arguably, for the new ways of working, the new mantra may need to be "Talent, talent, talent". Significant demographic changes are occurring in the global workforce. Skills in digital technology, automation, and artificial intelligence will be an important prerequisite for success in most organizations. However, the skills required of employees to meet the challenges ahead are under increasing pressure. Businesses are increasingly prioritizing ways for developing and maintaining key talent, for example, through competitor or supplier acquisitions, trying to identify and incubate hidden talent in their own workforces and exploiting technology to enhance collaboration. Additional considerations include the increasing benefits and needs of incorporating flexible working models and diversity into the talent mix. A war for talent is waging, and it shows no sign of abating. Victory will go to those organizations most successful at innovation, planning, prioritization, and follow-through in talent development and retention.
- **"Active engagement counters disengagement":** There is an obvious premium edge in having an engaged workforce. However, unless carefully managed, the forces we have discussed can readily lead to disengagement. People's attitude toward work is changing. Millennials, and more recently Gen Zs, are entering the workforce with quite different expectations around inclusion,

values, work-life balance, individuality, and mobility. Their numbers are building and we will be increasingly asking them to operate in an environment of permanent and substantial change. Yet they are also typically harder to please and to retain. They want their jobs to have meaning, and they want to feel that what they do matters. They want to feel engaged and, regardless of age, want leadership interactions that are transparent, fact-based, authentic, timely and personalized. They want to feel that they are valued and listened to. The new ways of working need to factor in active people engagement in order to counter what will otherwise be a high risk of disengagement and talent loss.

For most businesses, these changes will challenge many traditional structures, teaming models, comfort zones, and cultural norms. The edge will go to those organizations that excel at gaining new insights from an ever-changing business environment and can quickly respond with the right decisions, actions and adjustments to both strategy design and delivery. There are no cookie-cutter solutions. Success will not come easily, and will never be able to be taken for granted, but herein is a key element of the future basis for competitive advantage. Organizations will need to experiment and adjust. They will need to launch both integrated and discrete initiatives to build the operating model, structures, aligned leadership behaviours, integration mechanisms, talent, and culture to win. The people considerations need to be every bit as much in the foreground, and closely integrated with, the technology considerations.

This serves as a natural segue to our second topic. Specifically, how to think about those initiatives needed by companies to adapt to and win in the changing environment, both at the overall portfolio level and at the initiative by initiative level. Once again it is worth remembering 75 per cent of major transformations fail. Getting the component initiatives set up for success is a powerful means to flip these odds around.

Flipping the odds in favour of success

We now would like to share with you, DICE, a simple intuitive framework and tool that has proven its worth in rapidly assessing whether critical change initiatives are set up for success, failure or indeterminate outcomes. As a result, DICE helps identify the means for identifying and turning likely failures into successes – often prior to the initiatives even being launched.

Our research at the Boston Consulting Group and practice with clients worldwide shows that by rigorously focusing on four critical elements in each of the key initiatives , organizations can load the odds of in favour of success.

Duration, Integrity, Commitment and Effort – what we label the DICE factors – help predict the outcome of any transformation initiative. Working with companies engaging in ambitious change programmes, we have evolved the DICE framework which provides a common language for change and allows companies to tap into the insight and experience of their employees. This standard, quantitative and simple framework, enables the frank conversations needed about strategic change initiatives in order to surface and powerfully address critical issues and flip the odds in favour of success. The DICE framework is agnostic to the delivery method chosen and has proven its worth in both waterfall, agile and hybrid delivery models.

Now, let us consider each of the DICE factors:

1: Duration

Perhaps the most asked question in any change endeavour is 'How long is this going to take?' The assumption is that the longer something stretches into the future, the more likely it is to hit the corporate buffers. For organizations – and executive careers – there is little worse than a long-drawn out failure.

In fact, our studies at BCG show that the real issue executives should be worrying about is how often and how rigorously they review a key project for its progress and to identify any emerging issues that need course-correction. A lengthy project which is subject to regular, rigorous and issues-focused reviews is more likely to succeed than a project which is short in duration, but not regularly or effectively reviewed.

The key consideration is not the total duration of a project, but the time between properly structured and time effective reviews. The question executives should be asking is, 'How regularly and effectively are we going to be reviewing this?'

Our experience suggests that monthly reviews are the minimum level. If projects are allowed to progress beyond eight weeks without a review then the risks of encountering trouble increase exponentially. More complex projects require more frequent reviews – perhaps every two weeks.

Integral to having effective reviews is defining a set of milestones which provide senior leadership with a basis for operational insight into how a critical initiative is progressing. Of importance is that the milestones are written for the purposes of providing senior leadership with clarity on progress. Collectively these milestones constitute in effect a "roadmap" for a critical project, as such they are distinctive from the typical main activities on a project plan. There are usually 15 to 25 milestones per initiative that will be updated for progress on a monthly basis by the initiative owner.

The milestones describe the major intended actions or achievements within explicit time frames and include leading indicator metrics to assess the drivers of critical risks, and that the planned delivery of major interdependencies remains in scope and on time. The milestone dates serve as triggers for this forward looking testing and assessment. Practically this results in potential show stopper issues being elevated to senior leadership much sooner than would typically be the case, and at a stage when senior leadership are more likely to be able to make a difference – particularly through fast tracking decision making, removing roadblocks, resolving silo issues, and adjusting resource levels. Milestones also need to describe the financial and operational metrics that the project is expected to meet.

This not only ensures that the critical initiatives are built around the right actions and measures – that is, that the organization is doing the right things – but also that there is absolute clarity and accountability for delivering the expected business impacts. And, that based on regular updates from the initiative team leader (and likely the sponsor), there is a basis for sufficient operational clarity on progress and any emerging issues to support senior executives in being effective in their leadership roles during the implementation effort.

This is an obviously serious undertaking. It requires formal meetings (typically monthly) during which senior management, the sponsor and the project leader discuss a key project's performance on the dimensions that have a bearing on success and failure. The team must provide a concise report of its progress against milestones and attached metrics, and any risks or roadblocks that may be emerging.

2: Integrity

Any project is a human endeavour and a group effort. This requires what we describe as (team) performance integrity: a highly motivated and thoughtful project team with a bias for action, clear on its objectives, with a strong leader and sufficient member resources and the right mix of skills for the effort.

Team performance integrity is never perfect. No team in any organization is universally great all of the time. And there are always issues which can get in the way of the best possible team being fielded. For example, star performers are often prevented from joining change efforts because of the fear that their regular work will suffer. But fielding the best possible teams against the most critical initiatives is essential, the best outcomes in team establishment usually come from robust and structured leadership debate over trade-offs of between personnel "for running the business versus changing the business".

The demands of change are many, varied, and relentless. Project teams encounter a wide range of activities, resources, pressures, external stimuli, and unforeseen obstacles. This demands cohesion and leadership. The selection of the team leader and the team's composition is critical. The roles, commitments, and accountability of each team member must be clearly established.

In selecting the team leader, it is important to remember that effective managers of the status quo aren't necessarily adept at changing organizations. Good team leaders usually have problem solving skills, are results orientated, methodical in their approach but tolerate ambiguity, are organizationally smart, willing to accept responsibility for decisions, and, while being highly motivated, don't crave the limelight. Change demands heightened leadership capabilities.

As for the team, selection needs to be inclusive. Savvy leaders solicit names from key colleagues; by circulating criteria they have drawn up; and by looking for top performers in all functions. While they accept volunteers, they don't solely choose endorsers and proponents of the change initiative. It is important that senior executives personally interview people so that they can construct a team with the right portfolio of skills, knowledge, and social networks. They need also to make public the parameters by which the team's performance will be measured and how that evaluation fits into the company's regular appraisal process.

3: Commitment

The third DICE factor is commitment. Organizations need to maximize the commitment of two different groups of people if they want critical change projects to take root: They must get visibly, robust and aligned backing from the most influential executives (the DICE dimension we refer to as (C1). And they must take into account the enthusiasm – or often, lack thereof – of the people who must deal with the new systems, processes, or ways of working, (C2).

Top level commitment is vital to engendering commitment from those elsewhere in the organization. If employees don't see that the company's leadership is backing a critical project that they realize will significantly impact the business, how customers are served and most importantly their team and themselves, then they are unlikely to respond positively, far less change their own behaviours. No amount of top level support is too much.

Sometimes, senior executives are reluctant to back initiatives. This is probably more understandable than it might first appear. Resistance to change is only human. They are often bringing about changes that may negatively affect some employees' jobs and lives. But, if senior executives do not unequivocally communicate with one voice the need for change, and what it means for employees, they endanger the likely success of any project.

Second, organizations must take into account the skepticism – or often, lack thereof – of the people who must deal with the new systems, processes, or ways of working.

Despite repeated calls in the change management and leadership literature to engage with people, companies often underestimate the role that managers and staff play in transformation efforts. By communicating with them too late or inconsistently, senior executives usually end up alienating the people who are most affected by the changes. It's surprising how often something senior executives believe is a good thing is seen by staff as a bad thing, or a message that senior executives think is perfectly clear is misunderstood. This is normally due to senior executives communicating slightly different versions of critical messages.

There are two common communications traps that executives need to avoid: "We haven't got anything to say yet so it's not worth wasting people's time or worrying them" and "There is so much uncertainty and things in play that for now we are better off saying nothing until things become clearer". Getting caught in either of these traps inevitably requires a lot more leadership effort to get out of them than avoiding them in the first place.

Although it is an over-simplification, "the rule of three and nine" can serve as a useful guide for senior leaders in engaging employees and demonstrating commitment. It is more helpful than simply saying "you can never communicate enough". Specifically, leaders should communicate three times more than seems instinctively reasonable to them in order to effectively communicate during a time of major change. And employees usually need to hear a message nine times for them to realize that it actually relates to them and to understand what it means for them.

An interesting related point is that organizations routinely underestimate their ability to build staff support. A structured effort to reach out to employees can often turn a surprising number of them into champions of new ideas. Seek to engage people and they will usually discover a willingness to be engaged.

4: Effort

Change always requires extra efforts by people throughout the organization. The impact of this is often overlooked. But, the reality is that hard-pressed and hardworking people require convincing that any process of change is necessary and likely to benefit the organization and themselves.

At a practical level, it is important that the amount of extra work required of people is calculated rather than vaguely estimated with a promise of a better tomorrow. Ideally, no one's workload should increase more than 10 per cent in support of embedding a new change initiative. People become overstretched; resistance rises; and morale falls. Of course for many important change initiatives, the additional workload on staff to clear the hump of implementation and embed a new initiative (or often several related initiatives) and the consequent new ways of working will often significantly exceed 10 per cent. Here the other elements of DICE need to help take the load of offsetting the delivery risk. For example through boosting actions around senior leadership commitment (C1) and translating that into additional actions and interventions to garner local commitment (C2) in terms of why the change needs to occur and supporting people through the changes. The delivery team (I) needs to be that much more on the ball in terms of designing it and structuring the intitiative(s) in the best possible way and effectively engaging with critical local stakeholders.

In terms of the effort required, organizations need to have a clear sense of what is important to do and why as part of the change programme. It will be even more crucial to think through what not to do anymore, especially for those employees who will be playing a key role in the change programme, to balance existing responsibilities with new ones.

The previous example, in the discussion of Effort and how (I), (C1) and (C2) can interplay to offset a deficit in E, surfaces an important point. While we treat them distinctively, the components of DICE are not entirely independent. They can significantly influence and interplay with each other. For example superior senior leadership commitment (C1) is more likely to result in senior leaders driving to ensure that teams get the best possible resources (I).

The elements of DICE and the consequent environment they create makes instinctive sense. An initiative with a well-structured timeline and clear metrics, led by a great team with strong senior leadership commitment and highly committed local staff, who will only be required to put in a small amount of effort to support the introduction of a critical initiative is clearly likely to succeed. On the other hand, the opposite conditions suggest almost certain failure. The reality is that most initiatives are launched at neither of these extremes, they fall somewhere in between. The robust statistics behind the DICE equation enables the likely outcome to be determined based on the DICE database of the experiences of other organizations faced with comparable DICE conditions. That is why DICE and the conversations it generates are so powerful.

The DICE equation enables organizations to quantitatively determine if their change initiatives will succeed. This is done by asking executives to calculate scores against the DICE elements for each of the critical initiatives These scores are then combined to create an overall DICE score for each initiative. The calculation is very simple to complete. The score will range from 7-28 and predicts whether a project is set up for success, failure or an indeterminate outcome. In turn this rapidly fosters the right conversations on what interventions are needed to flip the odds in favour of success.

Our original analysis and development of DICE and the DICE equation was completed in 1994. In the years since then we have used DICE to help assess the likely outcomes, gain agreement on how to improve the odds of success, and help guide the execution of many thousands of change management initiatives worldwide. Across industry and across geography, the statistical correlation behind the DICE formula has held true and organizations' use of DICE has materially improved outcomes. DICE has also transitioned very successfully between different delivery methods. Be it waterfall, agile or a hybridized approach, the application of DICE has proven to readily predict and help enable the adjustment of outcomes in favour of success.

Of course, the assessments of the DICE factors are subjective, but DICE provides organizations with an objective and statistically rigorous framework in order to make decisions. And, it provides a lingua franca of change as well as serves as a vital catalyst for frank discussion and debate. We believe DICE offers the hard truth of change.

Further reading and information

For full information on the DICE framework please refer to Harold L. Sirkin, Perry Keenan and Alan Jackson, "The Hard Side of Change Management", *Harvard Business Review*, October 2005.

To learn more about calculating DICE scores and access to further support materials visit www.dice.bcg.com.

About the authors

Perry Keenan (keenan.perry@bcg.com) is a senior partner and managing director in the Chicago office of The Boston Consulting Group. He is a BCG Fellow, having previously led BCG's Change Management topic globally for ten years.

Jeanne Kwong Bickford (bickford.jeanne@bcg.com) is a senior partner and managing director in the New York office of The Boston Consulting Group. She leads the firm's Change Enablement Center and is head of BCG's New York office.

Peter Tollman (tollman.peter@bcg.com) is a senior partner and managing director in the Boston office of The Boston Consulting Group. He is a BCG Fellow, having previously led BCG's People and Organization practice in the Americas and the firm's biopharmaceuticals sector globally.

Grant Freeland (freeland.grant@bcg.com) is a senior partner and managing director in the Boston office of The Boston Consulting Group. He is the global leader of The Boston Consulting Group's People & Organization practice.

Resources

Vikram Bhalla, Susanne Dyrchs and Rainer Strack, "Twelve Forces that will Radically Change How Organizations Work", Boston Consulting Group, March 2017.

Perry Keenan, Jeanne Bickford, Annabel Doust, Jennifer Tankersley and Chris Johnson, "Strategic Initiatives Management", Boston Consulting Group, November 2013.

Perry Keenan, Stephanie Mingardon, Harold Sirkin and Jennifer Tankersley, "A Way to Assess and Prioritize your Change Efforts", *Harvard Business Review*, July 2015. https://hbr.org/2015/07/a-way-to-assess-and-prioritize-your-change-efforts

Perry Keenan, Jeanne Bickford, Jennifer Tankersley and Annabel Doust, "Pulse Executive Sponsor Engagement", Project Management Institute, October 2014.

Perry Keenan, Stephanie Mingardon, Jeanne Bickford, Tapio Schrey, Trish Clancy and Annabel Doust, "How to Ensure Your Change Efforts Stay on Track", Boston Consulting Group, March 2017. https://www.bcg.com/expertise/capabilities/change-management/how-ensure-change-efforts-stay-on-track-rigor-test-roadmap.aspx

Lars Faeste, Jim Hemerling, Perry Keenan, and Martin Reeves, "Transformation, the Imperative to Change", Boston Consulting Group November 2014.

Jim Hemerling, Diana Dosik and Shaheer Rizvi, "A Leader's Guide Always – On Transformation", Boston Consulting Group, November 2015.

Perry Keenan, Kimberly Powell, Huib Kurstjens, Michael Shanahan, Mike Lewis and Massimo Bussetti, "Changing Change Management", Boston Consulting Group, December 2012.

Yves Morieux and Peter Tollman, *Six Simple Rules – How to Manage Complexity without Getting Complicated*, Harvard Business Review Press, 2014.

Martin Reeves and Lisanne Pueschel, "Die another Day: What Leaders Can Do About the Shrinking Life Expectancy of Corporations", Boston Consulting Group, December 2015.

Fabrice Roghe, Andrew Toma, Stefan Scholz, Alexander Schudey and Jink Koike, "Boosting Performance through Organization Design", Boston Consulting Group, July 2017.

'INSTEAD OF TREATING EXECUTION AS SOMETHING THAT HAPPENS AFTER THE STRATEGY HAS BEEN SET, IT NEEDS TO BE BUILT INTO THE STRATEGY FROM THE START OR PEOPLE WON'T OWN IT.'

W CHAN KIM & RENÉE MAUBORGNE

STUART CRAINER & DES DEARLOVE

In search of strategy

Always start by defining terms. It sounds sensible and straightforward – especially with a subject like strategy, which has been studied from every angle.

But it is not.

In 1987 Henry Mintzberg offered five definitions of strategy for consideration: plan, ploy, pattern, position and perspective. Strategy is perhaps most commonly envisaged as a plan – consciously intended action developed in advance. A related concept is strategy as a ploy – a specific manoeuvre designed to outfox opponents. Strategy as pattern – the focus of much of Mintzberg's research – is a consistency of behaviour intended or otherwise. Strategy can be a position, an organization locating itself in an environment as Mintzberg describes it. This definition of strategy is consistent with the preceding definitions; an organization can position itself via a plan, a ploy, or as a pattern of behaviour. Finally, suggests Mintzberg, there is strategy as a perspective. In this instance it is effectively the ingrained perspective the organization has, it is collective and shared outlook on the world.

In *The Financial Times Guide to Strategy*, Richard Koch provides two senses for strategy:

"1. A good strategy is the commercial logic of a business, that defines why a firm can have a competitive advantage and a place in the sun. To be complete, a strategy must include a definition of the domain – the lines of business, types of customer and geographical reach – in which the firm competes. It must also include a definition of the firm's distinctive competencies and the competitive advantage that gives the firm a special hold on the chosen business domain.

2. Strategy also means what a company does, how it actually positions itself commercially and conducts the competitive battle. You can always attempt to describe a competitor's strategy, whether or not you think it sound. In this sense a strategy is what a firm does, not what it says it does, or what its strategy documents propound."

This provides some reassuring clarity, but also establishes that the scope of strategy is incredibly broad – from the logic of a business to what it actually does. And, as we shall see, the scope of strategy is ever broadening.

Costas Markides, the charismatic London Business School professor, provides this overview: "There is general agreement that every company needs a strategy – either explicit or implicit. Yet, there is surprisingly little agreement as to what strategy really is. Within both business and academic circles, it is not easy to identify two people who share the same definition of 'strategy'. Differences in opinion on the content and process of developing strategy are passionately argued. Yet these debates cease to matter when we realize two important points. First, strategy needs to be approached from a variety of perspectives. Second, rather than adopt a single perspective at the expense of all others, good strategies have to achieve a fine balance between seemingly divergent views.

"When it comes to strategy, I have found that there are three problem areas of controversy. I believe that sound strategic thinking achieves a fine balance between the arguments surrounding: (1) what constitutes the content and process of strategy, (2) strategy as analysis or creativity and (3) strategy dynamics. Analyzing each area in turn will help in achieving that fine balance.

"Strategy is both of these things: strategy must decide what game we want to play and then determine how to play that game well. As practised today, strategy is preoccupied with fixing the problems in the existing business rather than thinking about future businesses. The essence of a good strategy is to create new markets, new products and new industries. This leads to the position that strategy should be about competing for the industries of the future rather than competing for market share in the industries of today. It is hard to argue with the need to focus the organization's attention on discovering new markets. But this should not come at the expense of today's businesses.

"Therefore, the key question for any company is not whether it should try to create the industries of the future but how to take care of its existing business while at the same time attempting to create the industries of the future. Every company should also prepare for an unknown future — either by trying to create this new future itself or by creating the conditions that would allow it to exploit the future when it unfolds."

As these takes on strategy suggest, strategy really is a moveable feast, an awkward hybrid of delivery in the present and mapping out a persuasive future and route to get there. The challenge for all those charged with leading organizations is to reach their own definition of what strategy is and what it should do. Without this as a starting point, strategy is as useful as whistling in the organizational wind.

Key questions

At the heart of strategy is the ability to create a plan of action, which will lead to victory – whatever victory is thought to be in this instance. But, before the strategy is created a more basic question needs to be asked. "The strategist's method is very simply to challenge the prevailing assumptions with a single question: Why? and to put the same question relentlessly to those responsible for the current way of doing things until they are sick of it," explains Kenichi Ohmae in *The Mind of the Strategist*.

Before setting off it is worth returning to first principles and asking some vital questions. Like these:

1: Where are you?

The starting point must be a solid understanding of where you are and the dilemmas you face. If organizations are not in touch with the reality of their situation – however depressing this may seem – they have no hope of moving forward.

2: Where do you want to be?

If you don't know where you want to be you are unlikely to get there. In pursuit of this starting point organizations throughout the world have developed mission statements. "Most companies do have a mission statement. About 99.9 percent are useless," observes Costas Markides. Mission statements are also, confusingly, known by a variety of other labels (strategic intent, core objectives, visions, etc.) but the end-result is usually remarkably similar. Blandness does not differentiate or motivate.

Mission statements are, or should be, a pithy explanation of why a company is in business, what it intends to achieve and by what methods. The exercise of distilling an organization's raison d'etre into less than 100 words is often useful in itself. However, the results are often fatuous in the extreme. Mission statements have become meaningless PR exercises, pinned on noticeboards, printed on corporate keepsakes and generally ignored by the people they aim to influence. "Many managers misunderstand the nature and importance of mission, while others fail to comprehend it at all," concluded Andrew Campbell and his co-authors in *A Sense of Mission*.

Though they might help to encapsulate an organization's goals, mission statements are not strategy. They are more accurately described as the potential end-result of strategy, the objectives of the organization. Indeed, Henry Mintzberg defines strategy as the embodiment of a company's visions.

Mission statements should be bold, but achievable, goals. It sounds straightforward, but the means of identifying these objectives is clouded by controversy.

3: What do you want to achieve?

Any statement of intent relies on some knowledge of what it is you wish to achieve. Michael Porter argues that what every company should aim to achieve is competitive advantage. It must be better than its competitors in some way.

This has led to the elusive and almost mythical notion of sustainable competitive advantage. (One of the most important strategy books of the past decade, by Columbia Business School's Rita McGrath, is entitled *The End of Competitive Advantage*.) In reality, any competitive advantage is short-lived. If a company raises its quality standards and increases profits as a result, its competitors will follow. Businesses are quick to copy, mimic, pretend and, even, steal.

The logical and distressing conclusion is that an organization has to be continuously developing new forms of competitive advantage. It must move on all the time. If it stands still, competitive advantage will evaporate before its very eyes and competitors will pass.

The dangers of developing continuously are that it generates, and relies on, a climate of uncertainty. The company also runs the risk of fighting on too many fronts. This is often manifested in a huge number of improvement programmes in various parts of the organization which give the impression of moving forward, but are often simply cosmetic.

Constantly evolving and developing strategy is labeled strategic innovation. The mistake is to assume that strategic innovation calls for radical and continual major surgery on all corporate arteries. Continuous small changes across an organization make a difference. "We did not seek to be 100 percent better at anything. We seek to be one percent better at 100 things," said Jan Carlzon when he was CEO of the airline SAS.

4: What needs to change?

Even major surgery has its compromises. More realistic than most, Kenichi Ohmae, says that a good business strategy "is one, by which a company can gain significant ground on its competitors at an acceptable cost to itself". He believes there are four principal ways of doing this:

    1. Focus on the key factors for success (KFSs). Ohmae argues that certain functional or operating areas within every business are more critical for

success in that particular business environment than others. If you concentrate effort into these areas and your competitors do not, this is a source of competitive advantage. The problem, of course, is identifying what these key factors for success are.

2. Build on relative superiority. When all competitors are seeking to compete on the KFSs, a company can exploit any differences in competitive conditions. For example, it can make use of technology or sales networks not in direct competition with its rivals.

3. Pursue aggressive initiatives. Frequently, the only way to win against a much larger, entrenched competitor is to upset the competitive environment, by undermining the value of its KFSs – changing the rules of the game by introducing new KFSs.

4. Utilizing strategic degrees of freedom. By this tautological phrase, Ohmae means that the company can focus on innovation in areas which are "untouched by competitors".

"In each of these four methods, the principal concern is to avoid doing the same thing, on the same battleground, as the competition," Ohmae explains.

5: What are you good at?

The phrase core competencies has now entered the language of management. In layman's terms, core competencies are what a company excels at.

Gary Hamel and CK Prahalad, who made the term famous, define core competencies as "the skills that enable a firm to deliver a fundamental customer benefit". Hamel and Prahalad argue that strategic planning is neither radical enough or sufficiently long-term in perspective. Instead its aim remains incremental improvement. In contrast, they advocate crafting strategic architecture. The phraseology is unwieldy, but means basically that organizations should concentrate on re-writing the rules of their industry.

6: What is the context?

Nothing in the corporate world exists in a vacuum. Formulating a mission or any set of objectives must involve a plethora of people, as well as consideration of the broader forces at work in and on the organization.

This process was neatly summed up by Peter Drucker in a 1994 *Harvard Business Review* article. Drucker argues that every organization has a theory of business – the assumptions on which it has been built and is being run. To create a "valid theory of business" requires four elements:

1. The assumptions about environment, mission and core competencies must fit reality.

2. The assumptions in all three areas have to fit one another

3. The theory of the business must be known and understood throughout the organization

4. The theory of the business has to be tested constantly.

Along similar lines, Kenichi Ohmae argues that an effective strategic plan takes account of three main players – the company, the customer and the competition – each exerting their own influence. The strategy that ignores competitive reaction is flawed; so is the strategy that does not take into account sufficiently how the customer will react; and so, of course, is the strategic plan that does to explore fully the organization's capacity to implement it.

7: How do your achieve your objectives?

Implementation is where most strategies fail. Success relies on matching an organization's resources, culture, structure and people to the strategies, which emerge from consideration of an organization's core competencies and the environment it exists in.

Of course, no list of questions provides a foolproof answer or set of answers. The challenge for any organization is to develop its own culture of asking questions and interrogating reality. Passive acceptance is the route to failure; robust, continual questioning the path to strategic success.

About the authors

  Stuart Crainer and **Des Dearlove** are founders of the Thinkers50 (www.thinkers50.com).

Resources

Gary Hamel, & CK, Prahalad, *Competing for the Future*, Harvard Business School Press, 1994

Richard Koch, *The Financial Times Guide to Strategy*, FT Prentice Hall, 2011

Costas Markides, *Diversification, Refocusing and Economic Performance*, MIT Press, 1995

JI Moore, *Writers on Strategy and Strategic Management*, Penguin, 1992

Kenichi Ohmae, *The Mind of the Strategist*, McGraw Hill, 1982

'NEVER GIVE UP, FOR THAT IS JUST THE PLACE AND TIME WHEN THE TIDE WILL TURN.'

HARRIET BEECHER STOWE

ESSENTIAL THINKER

Roger Martin

The former dean of the University of Toronto's Rotman School of Management, Martin is a strategy advisor to CEOs worldwide and the author of ten books, including Thinkers50 award winners *Playing to Win* (with AG Lafley, HBR Press, 2013) and *Getting Beyond Better* (with Sally Osberg, HBR Press, 2015). His new book *Creating Great Choices* (with Jennifer Riel, HBR Press, 2017) follows up on his 2007 bestseller *The Opposable Mind* (HBR Press).

Roger Martin (rogermartin.com) is best known for his work on integrative thinking, and design thinking, both concepts he helped to originate and develop.

Integrative thinking is the ability to balance two opposing ideas or models in order to create a third, more effective solution to a problem. Design thinking combines analysis and intuition to exploit existing knowledge and create new knowledge.

Martin's pioneering work with AG Lafley, CEO at Procter & Gamble, is documented in their bestselling 2013 book *Playing to Win: How Strategy Really Works*. The book sets out a highly practical, step-by-step process for creating a workable business strategy, and explains how the methodology was used to stunning effect, with real life examples at P&G. The book earned Martin and Lafley the 2013 Thinkers50 Distinguished Achievement Award for Best Book.

He is the co-author (with Sally Osberg of the Skoll Foundation) of *Getting Beyond Better: How Social Entrepreneurship Works* (2015). It helped them win the 2015 Thinkers50 Distinguished Achievement Award for Social Enterprise. His most recent book is *Creating Great Choices* (with Jennifer Riel, HBR Press, 2017).

IN CONVERSATION

Roger Martin

Among the most intriguing of Roger Martin's wide ranging work is his long-term collaboration with Procter & Gamble CEO AG Lafley. Lafley and Martin are the co-authors of *Playing to Win, How Strategy Really Works*. When we spoke in 2013 on the book's publication, we began by asking Roger Martin about the big idea behind the book:

The big idea is you can make strategy simple, fun and effective. I don't think many people would say their strategy process, the job of putting together a strategy for their company, is any one of those three things. AG and I have a belief that you can make strategy very simple, it can be enjoyable to do, and very effective, and so we wrote a book about what we did together to do that at Procter and Gamble.

Not many executives really have a definition of strategy that's helpful to them. And so they do lots of analysis, put together very thick documents that sit on shelves, quite famously, and it's because they haven't made a few key choices. What we distilled it down to, in our practice, is five key choices. If you make those choices you'll have a strategy. If you haven't made those choices your strategy is probably not worth having.

So how did the collaboration with AG Lafley come about?

When he took over as CEO of Procter, in June of 2000, he phoned me and said, we've got a lot of challenges and things we need to do, and I'd known him for about ten years prior to that, working on various projects at Procter, and he asked me would I work with him as sort of a counsellor and advisor on strategy. So we worked together for the entire time he was CEO and chair of Procter, and worked on instilling in P&G a discipline about strategy that he had always believed needed to be there. So we worked together, learned together, and thought we should share the results of that collaboration.

We think that the stories that we can tell about Procter, they're not just a consultant going in from the outside and interviewing some people; we actually did it, and did it together, in a real environment. So we think it has an authenticity to it that is maybe unique.

Tell us about the five questions and how they fit together.

The most important thing about the five questions is that they have to be answered together, in a way that reinforces one another. So each of the five questions actually isn't all that hard to answer on its own, it's a little bit harder to answer them in a way that fits together. But the first question is: what is your winning aspiration? So, what are you trying to accomplish with your strategy? If you don't have that sense of an objective then it is very hard to have a useful strategy.

Now, many companies will have highfalutin aspirations, but those are not then linked to the key choices, which we call the heart of strategy – so that's questions two and three, where to play, and how to win. So, given your aspirations, where do you want to play – whatever market space you're looking at – and then, once you've chosen that, how do you want to win where you've chosen to play? Then the fourth choice is what capabilities do I need to have, to build, to maintain, to win in the place I've chosen to play, so that I can achieve my aspirations? And then finally, the last of the five questions is, what management systems do I have to have in place so that I have the capabilities built and maintained, so that I can win where I've chosen to play, and meet my aspirations?

So it's those five questions that a company needs to answer to have a strategy. The good news is there's no reason why you can't describe that in five pages or less, so you don't need a thick deck of slides. Five pages will do it. In fact, you should be able to summarize it on one page. But the key is that the great strategies are ones where those five things fit together and reinforce one another.

Can you give us an example of that?

We talk about the example of Olay, and the transformation it went through from Oil of Olay, a slow-growing, low price product with an aging demographic. So that's the brand that we looked at, starting as AG took over the beauty category in the late 90s, but then continuing through his presidency. And we looked at that and said, what are our aspirations for the skincare category?

Well, it turns out that in beauty skincare is the biggest and most profitable category – a $50 billion business worldwide. Procter really wanted to get bigger in beauty. It already had shampoos and conditioners and a little fragrance business, but it wanted to make that very big. So rather than make it a little sideline where we had this $750 million brand, which was low price and not very important, the aspiration was to make skincare a centrepiece of a beauty strategy, by having a leading brand in skincare.

But then we had a look and asked the question, where were we currently playing? Well, where we were playing was with a product targeted at aging women, and our demographic was aging. We were in the wrinkle-prevention, wrinkle cover up category. And our product was sold for about $3.99 for one little bottle of pink fluid. So we said, well, is there another place to play that would open up opportunities for us?

We came to the conclusion that there was a demographic that was younger, women aged 35 to 49, who were observing the first signs of aging, and were interested in something that helped them with signs of aging, not just wrinkles, but drier skin, spots, blemishes and the like – what we came to call the seven signs of aging. So we said if we chose our market as being for these very skin-involved women, who are a younger demographic, then we would be going dead at the heart of the category.

And then we said, well, how can we win with these women? What we realized is that we had to dramatically raise the quality proposition of the product, to reposition it as a substitute for what they paid really big bucks for in the department store channel. To do that we had to work with our retail partners to create a kind of a section in the store that made it feel more like the department store channel, but was in the store that the buyer was in on a regular basis, and also didn't have the pressure of the salesperson at the department store trying to sell you more and more stuff.

And so we had to build capabilities – everything from better packaging, to better active ingredients. We had to build all sorts of relationships with the beauty editors in the magazines, to persuade them to take our product seriously, and we ended up launching Olay Total Effects. We also dropped the "Oil of" prefix and made it Olay. Olay Total Effects, at 18.99, which is a stunningly high price point. We moved from Oil of Olay at 3.99, to Olay Total Effects at 18.99, but it was positioned in a different place. So it was a different where, and a very different how to win. Some additional capabilities were built behind that, and it ended up growing at 10-15 percent rate for over a decade, and is now by far the biggest skincare brand in the world, and probably, it's hard to tell exactly, but probably one of the most profitable.

So it's a $2.5 billion and growing business now (2013), all because we set an aspiration, picked a different where, figured out exactly how you had to win, built the capabilities, and the management systems around that. And we believe that's doable in any business, as long as you're willing to address those questions and really have an aspiration for winning, rather than just playing. Before, we were just playing, and now we're winning.

It's not a linear process, is it? It's very much an iterative process, with one part informing the rest, reinforcing the others.

Yes. That's an important point. There are so many companies that I've observed make their strategy process very linear, and one of the expressions of that is starting out with a long and involved and often painful wordsmithing exercise about what's our vision and mission.

The reason that that takes so long, often, and there are so many fights, is it's really hard to tell what your aspirations should be until you know a little bit more about the where to play and how to win. So you might set your aspiration as something that you cannot find a where to play and how to win that meet it. But if you've already locked and loaded on it, and had this whole exercise where we've now got the new vision and we've got the new aspiration, it's hard to then say, oh-oh, we've got to go back. So what we say, when we're doing strategy is, set an initial aspiration, then see about a where to play, how to win. If you can't find a where to play, how to win that's consistent with that, maybe go back and revisit it. You can try to create an initial where to play, how to win, then ask, can we really build the capabilities to win in that way? Oh, maybe not quite. Okay, so we're going to have to tweak it a little bit.

So you're right. It's this iterative process where the key is to frame it that way, to not have everybody say, oh no this is terrible we've now got to go back and revisit. That's a good part of strategy. That's a great part of strategy. It's what makes strategy powerful.

Are we talking about prototyping strategy?

AG and I are both really interested in the world of design, and it borrows some from that. You prototype your strategy decision, and then you look back and say, based on what's happened when we've exposed the prototype to people, we say, oh, you know, that's sort of right, but not quite. And you have that attitude towards strategy, so it doesn't feel like failure, it feels like getting it better and better and better.

Another of the messages of the book is that strategy isn't just for people who are up in the boardroom; that everybody should be doing strategy. So, whether you're a brand manager or in charge of a business unit, you should be doing your own strategy. But also that strategy needs to be done in the context of what the company's trying to do, in the context of the corporate strategy. That's the nesting concept you describe – all the sub-strategies should fit together seamlessly?

Absolutely. The strategies should fit with each other at every level in a corporation. So at Procter and Gamble they have to make strategy decisions about where to play, how to win at the corporate level, at the beauty care level, at the skincare level, at the individual brand level. I encourage the people I work with, whatever level they're at, to ask the question, what is your aspiration for the part of this company that you are in charge of? Even if it's just one little department, what's the aspiration? What is your where to play, how to win choice?

I would even go so far as to say every single person in an organization would be wise to have a where to play, how to win as an employee. Job descriptions aren't so specific as put your left foot in front of your right foot. They sort of say, well, here's your job. And within that you have a lot of choices – where exactly am I going to focus my time? How am I going to do that in a way that creates all sorts of value?

Really, the only thing you have to think about in this nesting concept is your where to play, how to win had better reinforce and make more powerful the where to play, how to win choices of the unit above you, and the unit above that and the unit above that. It's a view that holds that it is unhelpful to think that the CEO makes all the strategy choices because he's way above you, high up in the organization, and you're down below, running a business, and you just execute it.

No. In our view where ever you are in the organization you have to make strategy choices too. If everybody felt that they have to make strategy choices I think corporations would work a lot better than saying we make the choices up above, and you people down there execute. It's not the way the world actually works, and it's not a helpful kind of conception of the corporation.

Where are we in the overall strategy debate? What's changed since Michael Porter's Five Forces?

One thing that's now a core theme is getting strategy to be effective. So it's one thing for academics to admonish companies to do strategy my way, or some way, or whatever, and then companies not doing strategy, and not finding strategy particularly helpful.

So there's one huge theme of making sure strategy is doable by companies; that they can address strategy questions and come to answers.

Then there are these theoretical kinds of debates. A big one has to do with competitive advantage. I think a lot of the debate is not all that helpful. It is obvious that competitive advantage exists in the world. It is also obvious that competitive advantage doesn't last forever. Nothing lasts forever. And if you're trying to say that there is no such thing as competitive advantage, think of all the high performing, super-normally profitable companies, who've maintained that for years and years and years. It's hard to say that's not competitive advantage.

So the question, to me, becomes, is there a thinking process that can help managers make decisions that produce advantage, to create high amounts of value for customers that enables you to make an attractive return, and opens up other possibilities to keep on renewing that? That's the fundamental question I ask. My view is, yes, there's a process of thinking that's more likely to get you answers. There's an intelligent process for identifying where to play, how to win, and if we make choices of that sort we will position ourselves in a way that gives us the opportunity to keep modifying that and enhancing it ahead of other people, so that we do have an advantage over a sustained period of time. It's not the same advantage, right; it actually could be different sorts of advantages over time. So if you look over a 50-year period, it may actually be a whole bunch of different sorts of advantages. But it's because we have a practice of asking a set of questions that keeps us ahead of the game, rather than simply reacting to changes.

The world isn't static. Strategy isn't static, but that doesn't mean there isn't a way of thinking about the fundamental questions in a way that keeps you ahead of the competition.

ROGER MARTIN

Letter to the CEO

Dear CEO

The most pressing challenge facing the CEOs of today's corporation is incursion into corporate decision making of data analytics, commonly referred to using the fashionable moniker 'Big Data.' The state of play is that data analytics is considered fully above reproach: something that modern CEOs simply must embrace. If a CEO doesn't show unqualified reverence for data analytics, it is assumed that the CEO is a Neanderthal and/or Luddite. What has changed is that data analytics has migrated from the fringes of CEO life to the very epicenter. It is now the hottest thing in business.

CEOs are increasingly faced with an endless string of well-meaning but unreflective data analytics enthusiasts telling them that the 'data prove that X is true' or the 'correct decision based on the data analytics is to do Y.' The absolutely dominant prevailing wisdom is that CEOs should thank the messenger profusely and affirm that the decision based on data analytics is right. CEOs should instead ask the messenger the following five questions:

Question 1: From what era does all data in the world come?
Answer: From the past. There is no data about the future – yet.

Question 2: What is the full extent of what data analytics tell us?
Answer: What has been operative in the past based on how the world has worked in the past.

Question 3: What is our implicit assumption each and every time we use data analytics to decide what to do going forward?
Answer: We implicitly assume that the future will be a direct extrapolation of the past. It will either identical to the past or an extrapolation of the observed past trend into the future.

Question 4: What is the probability of making choices to create a future that is different from the past using data analytics?

Answer: Zero. Data analytics has zero ability to chart out a course that is anything other than an extrapolation of the past into the future.

Question 5: What is the probability that making a choice about the future based on data analytics will turn out badly?
Answer: High. Last time I checked, frequently the future turns out to be unexpectedly different from the past – annoyingly so, in fact.

The strong likelihood is that the big data enthusiast will not be able to answer any of the five questions, be baffled by the nature of the questions, and declare the CEO to be 'anti-analytics.' But by asking the questions and insisting on answers that demonstrate that data analytics are appropriate for the situation in question – and data analytics is appropriate when the future is likely to mirror the past – the CEO will be saving the company from the modern day vandals.

Instead, CEOs need to use the only methodology that has ever been useful in making decisions about the future: first, imagine possibilities and second, pick the one for which the most compelling argument can be made. In deciding which is backed by the most compelling argument, CEOs should indeed take into account all data that can be crunched. But in addition, CEOs should also use imagination, judgment, and experience of numerous data points from the past that the data analysts wouldn't consider 'objective data' to decide in what way to shape the future – like all the great CEOs in the history of business have done.

In doing so, CEOs will have to accept widespread ridicule in their organizations among the legion of big data enthusiasts, who will say that their CEO lacks rigor and makes decisions on 'gut feel' and is 'old school.' But these enthusiasts are likely to be blind and to have never asked questions concerning the logical limits of their methodology. So CEOs need to stand strong and make decisions that can create a better future for their organization and for humanity.

Sincerely,
Roger L Martin

This letter first appeared in the Thinkers50 book, *Dear CEO* (Bloomsbury, 2017).

'THINK LIKE A MAN OF ACTION, ACT LIKE A MAN OF THOUGHT.'

HENRI LOUIS BERGSON

DEBORAH ROWLAND

The changing nature of change

Look outside and test the temperature. Financial austerity lingers after the most major global economic crisis since World War II; shock political outcomes have created Brexit and a Trump presidency; there are 2.6 billion smartphone users, and 6.1bn (80 per cent of the world's population) predicted to have them by 2020; 65 million refugees are fleeing from their strife torn homelands, an increase from 19.2 million in 2005; and acts of brutal terrorism have put fear onto the beaches of Egypt and into the heart of cities as far apart as Beirut, Baghdad, Istanbul, London, Manchester, Mumbai, Sydney, Paris, and Barcelona.

In this turning and turbulent world, such unpredictable, unstable, interconnected and dynamic conditions change the very nature of change.

First and foremost, change moves from being a one off programme that can be initiated, implemented, and then put aside as you return to a new stability; to an ongoing changing phenomenon, in which survival requires you to be in a continual state of adaptation to new contexts. For sure there will still be a need for set piece change, such as an acquisition, a new brand launch, or an IT system change. Yet the emphasis has now shifted from viewing change as an episode to acknowledging it is an endemic phenomenon. This switch from change to changing, from noun to gerund, places a high premium on leaders who can build change capability in their institutions and foster it as an ongoing emergent process. The primary task of top leaders in today's unpredictable world is not to come up with the definitive grand plan for the future, but to create in society the capacity to be constantly in innovation and adjustment, as today's solution can look quickly outmoded.

Second, it is clear that the world is increasingly a globally interconnected place, in which change no longer lies within your personal control. Be it a result of social media, technology innovation, global migration or geopolitical union (or uncoupling as in Brexit), it is far less easy today to isolate causality for an event to just one location. You try to pull up the plant yet see that its roots are extensively connected to its neighbouring beds. Systemic and complex issues require a commensurate type of response. In such a world, the leadership of change requires a willingness to collaborate across traditional boundaries and to see the world as a connected ecosystem, underpinned by a deep capacity to hold an appreciation for the whole of existence over the selective promotion of certain beliefs or interests.

Finally, the new disruptive nature of change sharpens our attention to its process and its consequence. Given the increasingly high cost of failing to adapt to today's changing context – including our planet's very survival – I believe it's no longer good enough for leaders to bring about change without equal consideration for how to implement it. Too often I see leaders only attend to what has to be done, without any consideration for how to bring this about. I will go even further and say it is irresponsible to be a leader today if you are not prepared to examine and adapt your own response to these changing contexts. How you do change fundamentally determines where you end up.

So, change is now ongoing, endemic and not directly controllable. As the price tag for failure becomes ever more expensive, leadership is the essential capability. I have repeatedly shown through my own research that high quality leadership is the single biggest determinant of successful change outcomes. Yet while the need to master it rises in importance, we are also repeatedly reminded that most change efforts do in fact fail as the inherent difficulties faced in their implementation remain. Somehow, we are not learning from the lessons of experience. Now, more then ever, is the time to rectify that.

About the author

 Deborah Rowland (deborahrowland.com) has led change in major global organizations including Shell, Gucci, BBC Worldwide and PepsiCo where she was Vice President of Organizational & Management Development. Her 2017 book, *Still Moving*, is based on groundbreaking research into the realities of managing change.

'YOU CAN BE VERY BOLD AS A THEORETICIAN. GOOD THEORIES ARE LIKE GOOD ART. A PRACTITIONER HAS TO COMPROMISE.'

WARREN BENNIS

SHAMEEN PRASHANTHAM

Dancing with gorillas

Today's most pressing challenge for CEOs in diverse industries is that of coping entrepreneurially with the disruption being wrought by high-velocity technological advancements such as the digitization of economic activity and the convergence of previously distinct technologies. (How many predicted that the once-largest mobile phone company in the world, Nokia, would be disrupted by a computer company?)

Broadly speaking, CEOs who are vigilant to the need for continuous and rapid innovation have a two-pronged approach to foster entrepreneurship: from an internal perspective, they seek to promote intrapreneurship (that is, entrepreneurial efforts such as developing new products by existing employees) and investment in external entities, in some cases new ventures, often through minority stakes as a means of scanning the environment for new technological developments relevant to the corporation's strategy.

These efforts, which certainly have their uses, are insufficient because they tend to fall short in respect of accessing novel knowledge speedily. Intrapreneurship, by definition, involves internal employees whose skillset may reflect what the corporation already knows. Investment in startups often entails minority stakes and therefore an arm's-length engagement that is not particularly conducive to speedy fine-grained knowledge exchange. Yet, the high velocity of change in the technological environment warrants greater urgency in accessing novel knowledge from external firms – without necessarily having to control them.

Key questions CEOs should be thinking about are: How can we systematically partner with relevant innovative startups (before they disrupt us)? How can we synergize the impact of startup partnering with our other existing initiatives such as intrapreneurship and investing in external firms? How can we tap startup-rich knowledge pools around the world?

The solution entails a three-fold strategy:

First, corporations must develop capabilities and practices for systematic partnering with relevant innovative startups. An important facet of this is clarifying synergies between the corporation and startup-partners (for instance, distinguishing between product-building by the startup on top of the corporation's underlying platform technology versus solution-building by the startup to address pain points of the corporation).

Another aspect is creating interfaces that make partnering more user-friendly for the startup through the availability of designated "startup engagement managers" who represent a first port of call to startups and run well-defined practices such as boot camps, accelerators and go-to-market programmes.

Finally, a key element of systematic partnering is cultivating exemplars (success stories of startup partnerships) that serve as an inspiration for startups to partner with the corporation – which is likely to be competing with other corporations for the hearts and minds of innovative startups.

Second, corporations must harness value from their startup partnering in conjunction with their other entrepreneurial efforts such as intrapreneurship or investment in promising firms. While the limitations of initiatives pertaining to intrapreneurship and investment should be recognized, these are still of value to corporations. And, this value can be magnified through synergies with partnering initiatives targeted at startups. For instance, a partner-startup's new technology might be usefully integrated with a new idea emanating through an intrapreneurship programme to provide genuine novelty to the resultant innovative output. Or, partner-startups could be proactively viewed as prospective targets of investment – which means that invested startups will have more intimacy with the corporation than if they were merely the recipient of arm's-length investments.

Unfortunately, however, accomplishing such synergies is easier said than done because these initiatives are often carried out within organizational silos by managers who don't always talk to each other because of the organizational structure, or turf wars. What are required are boundary-spanning managers who are incentivized to nurture links across these initiatives.

Third, corporations must adopt a global mindset and adapt startup partnering practices to different contexts around the world. Of note are the differences between advanced and emerging markets. Corporations in advanced economies would be missing a trick if they overlooked the exciting innovation coming out of emerging markets – long seen as sources of low-cost labour with copycat firms. However, engaging with the small but distinct minority of startups interested in developing genuine intellectual property in markets like China and India will need modified partnering practices. For instance, corporations may have to work harder at partner screening to compensate for the lack of reliable benchmarking standards. As another example, corporations will typically have to build closer government ties to leverage policy efforts targeted at startups that have a heightened impact in such markets.

In conclusion, partnering with startups may have a cool ring to it, but doing it well calls for genuine commitment and considerable diligence. But the payoff will be worth it – unlike some of your disrupted competitors, you'll live to tell the tale.

About the author

 Dr. Shameen Prashantham is Associate Professor of International Business and Strategy at CEIBS. Prior to that, he worked at Nottingham University Business School China from 2011 and 2015 as Associate Professor in International Business & Strategy. He is the author of *Born Globals, Networks and the Large Multinational Enterprise: Insights from Bangalore and Beyond* (Routledge, 2015).

'STRATEGY IS NOT THE CONSEQUENCE OF PLANNING BUT THE OPPOSITE: ITS STARTING POINT.'

HENRY MINTZBERG

IN CONVERSATION

David Marlow

David Marlow is Company Transformation lead at Bristol-Myers Squibb. He explained more about his role and the nature of transformation in conversation with Stuart Crainer.

Being responsible for the company's global transformation management office is a big job.

It's a very interesting role. I report to the Chairman and CEO of the company. He personally asked me to help with the development and execution of the overall plan. It's motivating and a huge learning opportunity.

What are your foundation beliefs about how transformation works, or needs to work, in a global company like BMS?

The first thing to realize is that strategy on its own won't transform an organization. The second element is culture. If you put strategy and culture together that will equal success. The culture element needs a similar weighting to the strategy element. People create and evolve the culture of an organization, its DNA. Strategy is the *what* and the people side of the equation is the *how*.

One thing I see people struggling with in organizations is the new normal of constant change. This is driven by the external environment where there is a huge amount of activity – think of the rise of political uncertainty, the growth of the digital economy and so on. Internally you can dial up or down the change component in terms of your specific needs, areas of focus and what you want to prioritize. But the point is that constant change is here to stay. So how do you equip the leaders and employees of the company to not only manage the change, but also to flourish in it? I think of this in a positive way as embracing change and how you drive an organization to be ready for any change. It is a matter of becoming a resilient organization, but also one characterized by agility, the ability to act very quickly depending on how these constant change issues come at you.

Another component is change fatigue. It is not so much the physical side of the equation – working 12 hours rather than ten hours today – it is the emotional component. All of these things have an impact on the emotional well-being of employees. I'm used to working a lot of hours, but sometimes I feel like a sponge under a leaking tap which is dripping constantly. You are continually absorbing negative energy from the rest of the organization as people complain that you are trying to achieve too much too soon, they can't do it and so on. All this negative energy comes your way so you have to step back, not take it personally, and take the opportunity to metaphorically ring the sponge out.

This emotional component to transformation people sometimes under-estimate. It is very easy to make decisions from a strategic perspective about what you want to do, but execution is always very challenging and has an emotional component.

What are the other key elements of making transformation a reality rather than simply a strategy?

First, to drive successful strategy implementation it has to be leader led. There has to be a personal commitment from the CEO of the company. The whole management team at the most senior level of the company must have a personal commitment to make the transformation work.

Second, there needs to be clarity around where you are as an organization and where the organization needs to go and where it needs to grow. You have to be able to paint that picture and to articulate it consistently and appropriately to different levels – board level, senior management level and employee level.

Third, there has to be ruthless prioritization of the critical value drivers of what will be a multi-year programme. There has to be very tangible and specific objectives and accountability for who owns the value drivers.

You have to continually prioritize. There are always competing activities which are ongoing in any organization – the launch of new products, other initiatives in other parts of the company, different functions wanting to do things with a different view of what they want to prioritize. This requires you to look at the enterprise level, at the overall amount of activities that are going on, and do an initiative prioritization assessment once or twice a year. This makes sure you understand where the big value drivers are and that they are properly resourced and prioritized.

Fourth, communicate, communicate, and communicate. There are really tough parts of any transformation which you have to communicate. People, even at the leadership level, often don't like to talk about the less positive side of the transformation. It is easy to say that you're designing and creating a new organization, you're building new capabilities and that is a very important part of driving value. It is much harder to communicate that, to fund the transformation you have to cut back on resources in other parts of the organization, and you are going to let go of some of your colleagues. Of course, this is hard, but if you want people to come with you on the transformation journey you need to communicate with them constantly

Any person can deal with certainty but it is when there is uncertainty that there is a challenge. That is the nature of the beast. If you don't have certainty it creates a lot of churn. It is okay to say, 'This is what we know today, but we don't know this because we're still working on it. As soon as we know, we'll bring you into the loop and communicate in an open way.' That sort of open communication goes a long way.

Related to this, for me personally there are couple of North Stars which I think are key to me being successful in this role. The first is to stay true to the original design principles. If you put a huge effort into creating a vision of where you want to go, you need to stay true to that. People tend to make compromises or to start minimizing some of the bold thinking. This can cause a huge amount of value leakage from the programme. You have to be very disciplined about sticking to the original design principles.

The second personal thing for me is to treat people with respect and dignity. In transformation programmes there is a financial component and a workforce reduction element. You have to treat people fairly and with respect, you need to take into consideration the personal circumstances of people.

These are things that as the leader of this transformation are always in the back of my mind.

The final thing is to always put your best talent on critical initiatives and make sure that you reward them accordingly, but more importantly make sure that they will have roles after the completion of the assignment. If you compromise on that you will get a sub-optimal outcome. People are often very reluctant to free up talent so leaders have to provide people with the motivation to get involved and to offer them future opportunities to learn and grow.

What have you learnt in this role?

First, there is never a perfect plan, there are always bumps in the road. It's important to recognize that up front so that when the bumps arrive you have the right data and information to make an informed discussion around the topic and then conclude the best steps moving forward. At the same time you don't want to stifle the original bold inspirational thinking.

The second thing goes back to leader-led change: the CEO of any company has to appreciate that their decisions are vital in achieving success. They need to live with their decisions and not to become frustrated if the organization doesn't react as quickly or if different parts of the organization move at different speeds. Having said that, relentless focus and follow through is a must.

Is it easier to achieve transformation as an insider in the organization or does it require an external appointment?

When you are establishing the need for the programme, to establish and identify what the burning platform is, it is always useful to get an external perspective so that you can benchmark data or identify the latest trends in the industry and so on. Some of the big consulting firms, like BCG and McKinsey, have enormous databases and experience so it is useful to have some involvement from them in order to benchmark, to run ideation sessions and to understand what the programme could look like.

When it comes to implementation, it has to be a much more company-owned effort. Internal talent must be made available. You can always augment that with external resources – such as additional project managers or a communications specialist – if there is a very specific thing you want to implement which requires a subject matter expert which you don't have in house

During the phase including the benchmarking, ideation and coming up with aspirational goals you have to make sure that there is a good database and information trail. Consultants come and go so you have to be very sure and clear on the documentation which serves as a base for your programme. Data can be your biggest enemy or your best friend. Good data enables informed decisions and clarity on accountability. But, if you don't have good data people tend to hide behind it.

Is your finance background an advantage in this role?

I do have a finance background and have also been involved in mergers and acquisitions at my prior company. But I am not a traditional bean counter in that I have an enormous passion for people and culture. It is so important to have the right people and to be able to engage people. If you get the right team together – a diverse group of individuals who think very differently and who help each other – it is amazing what they can achieve.

When it comes to implementation it boils down to people – whether it is understanding their context, where are they in their careers or what motivates them. If you don't crack the people code transformation programmes do not succeed or will deliver suboptimal results.

Are you fighting against human nature in that people will never really have an appetite for change, especially continuous change?

People don't like change because it takes them out of their comfort zone. But, if there is a compelling business case for change people can rally behind it. For example, in our line of business we sometimes have huge patent cliffs. Overnight we can lose billions of annual revenue. There is huge unmet medical need for millions of patients across the globe. Up-investing in our R&D pipeline and speed to our patients require resource trade off choices. Those examples are very easy to explain to people.

It is much more difficult to start challenging a successful organization to have a continuous improvement mindset.

What stage is BMS in its transformation journey?

Let me separate that into the *what* and *how*. *What* covers what we want to do in the different parts of the organization and different parts of the organization are on different timelines their journey. In some areas you can achieve transformation very quickly. In others less so. When you are re-engineering entire processes, enabled by technology, in a global company these are multi-year marathons requiring different level of energy. You have to think about how you can engage people in a multi-year transformation.

A holistic transformation across the entire enterprise demands energy, focus and effort from the leadership in order to make sure the right outcome is achieved. And, if you don't put some metrics and governance in place there is the danger that things will creep back and then in a few years time you will be back where you started

The *how* is more difficult because that gets into the people side of the equation. Do you have the right capabilities starting at the leadership level? Where are you with the culture of the organization? Where are you trying to take it? You are always trying to advance your people investing in them, so culture change is ongoing, always. And it's important because it's what gets you sustainable results. Being purposeful about culture, defining it and modeling it at the top is critical. They key, too, is rewarding people, in big and small ways, for working in new ways that drive the new culture, and making it something you experience everywhere, all the time. Culture is *how* you get even greater results. It's not just the soft stuff, though many companies think of it that way. Culture is a critical component of strategic execution.

Finally, it is good practice to pause periodically and assess the initial vision for the transformation relative to actions taken and current trajectory, making course corrections as necessary.

'ACT QUICKLY, THINK SLOWLY.'

GREEK PROVERB

ESSENTIAL THINKER

Rita McGrath

Rita McGrath (ritamcgrath.com) is a Professor at Columbia Business School. She is the author and co-author (with Ian MacMillan) of a number of bestselling books. These include: *The Entrepreneurial Mindset* (Harvard Business School Press, 2000); *Market Busters* (Harvard Business School Press, 2005); and *Discovery Driven Growth* (Harvard Business School Press, 2008).

McGrath won the 2013 Thinkers50 Strategy Distinguished Achievement Award; and her most recent book *The End of Competitive Advantage: How to Keep Your Strategy Moving As Fast as Your Business* (HBSP, 2013) was shortlisted for the Thinkers50 Best Book Award. In it, she sounds the death knell for sustainable competitive advantage, observing that strategy and innovation are converging.

McGrath argues that it's time to go beyond the very concept of sustainable competitive advantage. Instead, organizations need to forge a new path to winning: capturing opportunities fast, exploiting them decisively, and moving on even before they are exhausted. She shows how to do this with a new set of practices based on the notion of transient competitive advantage.

Rita McGrath is founder of Valize (valize.com). Building on her research, Valize aims to help organizations build the capability to innovate by moving up the Innovation Maturity Scale.

Rita McGrath

The *End of Competitive Advantage* was a hugely successful book, and a real breakthrough book for you, but it's been a few years now, so what have you worked on since? What are you working on now?

Lots of different projects. I have a new book in the works which is about strategic inflection points. One of the interesting things in doing the research for this new book is that between the time an inflection point gets going and the time it actually shows up on your doorstep, typically you have time to act. That was the most interesting thing to me, which was that people always think inflection points come out of the ether and eat us alive, but usually they've been brewing for some time.

So, let me give an example. Back in two thousand and something, YouTube was created and it was created by a bunch of guys who were fed up with how difficult it was to share videos with one another. And in the beginning, nobody really took it seriously, because what was it? It was cat videos. Who could take that seriously? But if you think about it, with YouTube, for the very first time, any individual, anywhere, with a smart phone or recording device, could share video with millions of people. Before that invention you would have had to own a movie studio – you would have had to be Universal Talent or something – to do that. So, it relaxed a constraint for everybody.

At the same time you had, around then, the invention of Facebook. If you wanted to send a message to a billion people, before Facebook, you would have had to own printing presses. You would have had to own multiple media stations. After Facebook, you could send it instantly, and again, nobody took it seriously in the beginning, because what was it? College kids sending beer bong pictures around to each other. Nobody really thought it was a big deal.

And at the same time, around 2006, you had the invention of Amazon Webservices, and again, for the first time, two guys in a garage could harness the computing power that you would have had to be IBM to use years before that. So, you put those three things together, and what you've got now is this absolutely potent mix of being able to share a video, share content, and do it all in a flexible computer backbone, which had never been possible before. One of the companies that really took advantage of this is a company called Dollar Shave Club.

Mike Dubin, who started Dollar Shave Club, was basically ticked off at how difficult it was to supply his shaving needs. In America, for example, you have to go to a drug store, and because shaving razors are so expensive they're like catnip for shoplifters. And so, what they do is they keep them behind lock and key, inside a cabinet called "the shaving fortress."

You had to go find a helpful shop floor clerk and get them to unlock the shaving fortress and get your razors, and the last time I looked, a six pack of Gillette razors was something like $18.96. I mean they're really expensive.

And so, Mike Dubin said, why does it have to be that way? We can make high quality razors. We can source them from Korea, and we can send them to you, on your doorstep, once a month. So, that was a good idea, but what made it really take off, past the inflection point, was he made this hilarious two-minute video about how his razors were going to change the world, and then broadcast it. It went viral almost instantly.

People on Facebook became brand ambassadors. So, people at Procter and Gamble, for example, would have paid sales force to do it, but all of a sudden, Dollar Shave Club has all this free publicity, with hundreds of hits, 20,000 blades sold on the very first day this thing went live. Dollar Shave Club's now five years old and it is a very big, sustainable business. Unilever bought the company last July for $1 billion, so they had a very successful exit.

Procter and Gamble, their share of the men's cartridge market in the United States, went from about 71 per cent in 2010, to just under 60 per cent. It's about 59 per cent today, and totally took them by surprise. But this is my point about inflection points, which is, have you been paying attention? What constraint is being relaxed in the environment that I'm used to competing in? They could have possibly seen that, and they could have mounted a response earlier, rather than getting whacked by something that took them by surprise.

How do you define a strategic inflection point?

Any industry, any company, when you're operating within an envelope of constraints, which are dictated by the technology of the time, by what's possible at the time, and you grow up with that as part of your DNA. So years ago, all of publishing, for instance, was constrained by what's the cost of paper and ink? What are the union contracts around how we deliver and what we do? What are the constraints that limit how much reach we have? How much advertising we have? And yet, when something comes along that changes those constraints that has the seed of an inflection point, and because you're used to dwelling within this envelope of constraints, you don't even see it coming.

What's surprised you about the research?

Well, the surprising thing was how obvious it all is in hindsight. You look back and you say well of course, duh, we didn't see that. But in the moment, it's very hard, and I think part of it is what I call, the problem of the dance floor versus the balcony. If you go to a dance, and you're on the dance floor, and you're in the action and you're dancing and you're moving, and somebody were to ask you afterwards, what was it like? You would have said, it was fantastic. People wore great dresses and the music was loud, and I got to meet all these fascinating people. But if you had stopped the dance and gone up to the balcony, and looked down on the dance floor, you would have seen a completely different picture of what was going on that evening.

So, I think part of the message of the book is, we need to be able to do both. We can't just stay on the balcony. If you just stay on the balcony, you're not going to make anything happen, but if you're so enmeshed, and this is where I see so many executives today, being completely enmeshed in what's going on, what's the next email, what's the next meeting, what's the next airplane flight? And they really don't take that balcony perspective and step back and say, what's the bigger picture here?

And what's stopping them from doing that? Just the fascination with, or the obsession with action and doing things in the short term, or short-term financial pressures?

A lot of it is the way our financial system is set up – that's a whole other conversation. But there aren't a lot of incentives to take that balcony perspective in your ordinary executive's life. Their world is scheduled out for months sometimes. I've had people try to schedule meetings with chief executives, and they try to set up a meeting for when he's on a plane, but that meeting's already scheduled with six people. So, I think they're just so busy they don't realise that it takes time to step back and reflect, and see what the bigger picture really is.

And when you talk to CEOs and people in the C-suite, how do they respond to these ideas?

Three responses, one is, don't be ridiculous, that's not me. Two is, oh, I never thought about it that way, maybe I should think about it, and three is, yes, we have processes in place to regularly do this.

Do attitudes change? You travel a lot. Are there different attitudes in different countries?

Yes, I would say countries that are more stable, where there's less open competition tend to be less fluid. There's fewer of these inflection points coming and kicking you, because there is less opportunity for them to do that. But countries where the markets are more open are more likely to be affected. And if I think about the United States, one of the things that is very interesting is that you've got this juxtaposition of some industries, some sectors, which are becoming actually more oligopolistic. So, airlines, cable television, internet services, contrasted with some that are just wildly competitive, and it's fascinating to me that you've got this juxtaposition of the two in one economy.

Where will that go though? Is that sustainable?

I don't think oligopolies are. We were just talking about airlines earlier, and they're going to end up getting their levels of customer service regulated, if they're not careful, because the public is so annoyed at them.

But the other extreme, the wild west of competition, is that viable in the long-term?

It can be if competitors do it properly, but it is difficult. It shaves margins, it gets people thinking very much in terms of the next move, rather than the next strategy. So, that has its own problems.

You spend your time travelling the world, talking about these ideas, what do you enjoy about it? You need to spend an awful lot of time in airports.

You do. I love the people. I love hearing what they're thinking about, what they're worried about. I love learning from different environments. That's very rewarding to me. I think one of the things that myself, as well as the other thinkers that you work with, one of our great advantages is we get to talk to lots of different companies, and we actually get paid to think, which is astonishing. So, when you talk to people from different environments and say, hey, have you thought about this, have you thought about that? And their eyes light up and a light bulb goes on, that's very rewarding.

'THE ABILITY TO REINVENT PROFESSIONALLY AND ORGANIZATIONALLY IS ONE OF THE MOST IMPORTANT COMPETENCIES TO MASTER IN THE 21ST CENTURY. LEARNING HOW TO LEVERAGE AND ACTUALLY ACCELERATE RESULTS WHEN DISRUPTION HITS WILL BE A NEW SKILL THAT TOP COMPANIES WILL GROW AND LEARN.'

SHANE CRAGUN & KATE SWEETMAN

STUART CRAINER & DES DEARLOVE

How to succeed with strategy

1. Tune in: "Despite the roar of voices wanting to equate strategy with ambition, leadership, 'vision', planning, or the economic logic of competition, strategy is none of these. The core of strategy work is always the same: discovering the critical factors in a situation and designing a way of co-ordinating and focusing actions to deal with those factors," says Richard Rumelt.

2. Ask questions: You tune in by asking questions. Simple. "We need to ask better questions and generate fewer hypotheses -- to allow ourselves to be pulled by real-life concerns rather than pushed by reified concepts. We need better practice, not neater theory," advises Henry Mintzberg. "So we must concern ourselves with process and content, statics and dynamics, constraint and inspiration, the cognitive and the collective, the planned and the learned, the economic and the political. In other words, we must give more attention to the entire elephant – to strategy formation as a whole. We may never see it fully, but we can certainly see it better."

3. Understand the context: David Bach of Yale School of Management observes: "Companies are very comfortable with the idea that you can shape customers' expectations, erect entry barriers, change your relationship with suppliers, and mold your market environment. They are not so comfortable with the idea of trying to mold their social and political environment."

3. Think of barriers to exit not barriers to entry: In the past the strategic talk was of barriers to entry, but now we've got to start thinking in terms of barriers to exit. "I argue that one of the things firms are going to do differently is they're going to be much more careful about sinking lots of assets and lots of investment into specifically competitive places because if you need to move fast you don't want a lot of fixed assets," says Rita McGrath. "You want to be able to use assets that are fairly fungible. It's access to assets rather than ownership of assets, which we're going to see as the defining issue in how you expend resources going forward."

4. Look to create new markets: Mining existing markets is necessary but increasingly not sufficient to secure future growth. "The challenge is to create new demand, what we call new market space," says *Blue Ocean Strategy* co-author Renee Mauborgne. "New market space is about creating a company's future. Companies can continue to mine their wealth from an existing market space — that's maintenance. They can concentrate on market share. But there is something more — the act of creation. Creating new market space will become increasingly vital.

"Creating new market space provides growth. There are two paths to growth. One is the mergers and acquisition path, which often leads to growth but rarely leads to profitable growth. The other is organic growth by creating new businesses. While this path is profitable and necessary, in markets where supply exceeds demand, companies are often hesitant because they don't have a path forward to believe that they could succeed in changing things. They need a bridge to get there. Hopefully, some of the ideas and analytics we have been developing will help companies in building that bridge."

5. Involve as many people as possible: The C-suite doesn't have a monopoly on strategic wisdom – or any other kind of wisdom. People throughout an organization need to be emboldened to think and care about strategy. Says Roger Martin: "Where ever you are in the organization you have to make strategy choices too. If everybody felt that they have to make strategy choices I think corporations would work a lot better than saying we make the choices up above, and you people down there execute. It's not the way the world actually works, and it's not a helpful kind of conception of the corporation."

6. Know yourself: Leaders are encouraged to really understand their inner ambitions and motivations. Much the same applies to organizations. Success comes from within. Chris Zook of Bain told us that the consistent revelation of his research and case studies is that the main barrier to companies finding their next wave of growth is themselves. "The answer is internal," he advised. "Only 15 per cent of the variation in performance among companies is related to choice of market, and 85 per cent is related to how those businesses compete against others around them. And when we actually look at the main issues and barriers that companies have in that regard, we find more of them tend to be internal than external. Businesses can tend to be their own enemies, and self-awareness, at the end of the day, is probably at the epicenter of a lot of the great success stories and great failure stories in business." Look inside.

'THE MARK OF A GOOD ACTION IS THAT IT APPEARS INEVITABLE IN RETROSPECT.'

ROBERT LOUIS STEVENSON

ALEX OSTERWALDER & YVES PIGNEUR

Letter to the CEO

Dear CEO

A recent McKinsey study (McKinsey Global Innovation Survey) shows that 80 per cent of your CEO peers think that their current business model is at risk. The research also shows that a mere 6 per cent of your executives are satisfied with the innovation process in your organization.

You have been excellent at executing and improving your proven and successful business models. But as the research above shows, you have not yet found the answer to inventing entirely new business models, value propositions, and growth engines.

In fact, managing the present is taking oxygen away from inventing the future. To prevent this from happening you need a powerful Chief Entrepreneur to focus on the future while you focus on the present. You need to give these entrepreneurs prestige and power and a space for new ideas to flourish and thrive. And you need to change the way your organization is structured so it can systematically churn out new growth engines. Anything less than this is innovation theatre, and that's just not enough.

1. The leadership challenge: simultaneously manage the present and invent the future.

You're likely to be in your current position because you are world class at managing and growing the company's known business model. However, it's no longer enough to "only" be world class at execution. We like to say that business models and value propositions expire like a yogurt in the fridge. The reality is that business models are expiring faster than ever before. The likelihood of a CEO managing a single business model through his or her tenure no longer exists. You have to also invent the future, which will require systematically and continuously inventing new business models. You not only have to be world class at executing and improving your current business model, but you also have to be world class at searching and inventing new business models for the future.

That's the real leadership challenge.

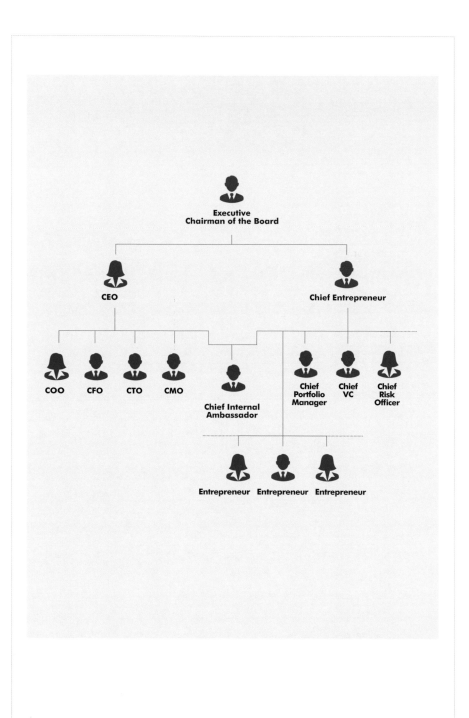

Innovation today is about exploiting market opportunities with new business models and value propositions. This does not mean pumping more money into R&D. Product and technology innovation – classic R&D – is not enough to keep you relevant. We can point to businesses like Kodak, Nokia, and Blackberry as warning signs of innovative technology companies that went bust. Instead, you have to allocate a percentage of your R&D budget to the exploration of business models and value propositions.

You would have to be schizophrenic, and have more than twenty-four hours in the day, to be world-class at both jobs. In order to excel at both, you need a powerful person skilled at execution who focuses on the present, and a powerful person skilled at entrepreneurship who focuses on inventing the future. You need to create an innovation engine that will function alongside your current business. This is a whole new organizational chart of people and skills led at the top by a Chief Entrepreneur.

This "ambidextrous culture" is how you will survive in the 21st century.

2. What does an innovation engine do?

Your innovation engine is a home for the entrepreneurs inside your business. It's where new growth engines are manufactured and it's managed by a Chief Entrepreneur. It's a space where new business ideas can flourish and thrive. It's a space for new ideas that are very different, or potentially in conflict, from the established business model.

Your innovation engine is not a space where you write business plans for new ideas. Your main goal is to decrease the risk and uncertainty around new ideas. It's a space where you prototype and test new business models and value propositions; where you experiment and gather evidence as cheaply and quickly as possible by getting out of the building with methodologies like Lean Startup and Customer Discovery.

It's a myth that innovation is extremely risky and costly – in fact, innovation is only an expensive gamble when you do it wrong. Today the knowledge, tools and processes exist to systematically reduce the market risk inherent to new ideas, business models, and value propositions.

The use of visual and practical tools like the Business Model & Value Proposition Canvas will help you shape, prototype, and test new business ideas systematically – similar to how architects design new buildings. These tools encourage teams to design quick and rough prototypes that can be tested on customers immediately for fast feedback and learning.

3. The challenge has changed, and so the organization needs to change.

The challenge is that companies need to constantly churn out new business models. Not just new business ideas--but entirely new growth engines year over year. This is a crucial turning point for 21st century organizations, and it requires a new organizational model to address the challenge of constantly churning out new growth engines.

Do you have the organizational structures in place to be world class at executing, but also at churning out new growth engines? On one hand your execution engine will need to be world class at managing factories and tolerating zero failure; and on the other hand, your innovation engine will need to be world class at experimenting, failing, and learning to shape new ideas.

Lastly, your innovation engine will need help from your execution engine--we cannot stress this enough. You need to give entrepreneurs the advantages of a large company. You have to give them access to existing brand credibility, existing customers, existing resources and assets that can be powerful for the innovation engine's exploration of new growth engines. This is what distinguishes internal ventures from startups.

Very few companies are good at this ambidextrous culture, but this is changing. Companies are slowly and steadily acting in the face of business model disruption. This is going to be a difficult journey, but you are not alone in this challenge. The truth is, there's never going to be a right time to start. If you don't want to end up like Kodak, Nokia, or Blackberry, then you have to start now.

Sincerely,
Alexander Osterwalder & Yves Pigneur

About the authors

Alexander Osterwalder & Yves Pigneur are winners of the 2015 Thinkers50 Distinguished Achievement Award for Strategy. They are the authors of the international bestseller *Business Model Generation: A Handbook for Visionaries, Gamechangers and Challengers* (Wiley, 2010). They have also written a string of other books, including: *Value Proposition Design: How to Create Products and Services Customers Want*; *Business Model You: A One-Page Model for Reinventing Your Career*. They are Thinkers50 ranked thinkers.

This letter first appeared in the Thinkers50 book, *Dear CEO* (Bloomsbury, 2017).

'MEN OF ACTION WHOSE MINDS ARE TOO BUSY WITH THE DAY'S WORK TO SEE BEYOND IT. THEY ARE ESSENTIAL MEN, WE CANNOT DO WITHOUT THEM, AND YET WE MUST NOT ALLOW ALL OUR VISION TO BE BOUND BY THE LIMITATIONS OF MEN OF ACTION.'

PEARL S BUCK

RICARDO VIANA VARGAS & EDIVANDRO CONFORTO

Great strategies need great delivery: The 10 principles of implementation excellence

Every CEO or leader is accountable for overseeing strategy design and delivery in his or her organization. Leaders also recognize that strategy implementation excellence is central to the organization's sustainable growth and prosperity. Yet most strategic initiatives fail because of flawed implementation, at great cost in time and resources. Consider these data points:

- A full 90 per cent of respondents to a 2017 global survey of 500 senior executives from companies with annual revenues of over $1 billion, conducted by the Economist Intelligence Unit (EIU), admitted that they failed to reach all of their strategic goals because of flawed implementation.
- More than half (53 per cent) of respondents to the EIU survey admitted that ineffective implementation of strategic initiatives has a profound impact on the organization's competitive advantage and performance.
- In addition, the Project Management Institute's Pulse of the Profession Survey found that for every $1 billion invested, $97 million is wasted through poor implementation performance.

Mind the strategy implementation gap

Global competition and a networked society are driving almost daily changes in the competitive landscape. In this highly kinetic environment, sustainable growth will depend on delivering the right strategies the right way. Yet the average organization fails to meet at least 20 per cent of its strategic goals as the result of implementation issues and challenges, according to the 2017 EIU survey. An earlier EIU study, published in 2013, showed that just a little over half of the strategic initiatives (56 per cent) have been successful.

The dynamic interplay between strategy design and delivery starts at the moment the organization defines its strategic goals and investments. Most organization leaders appear to understand the importance of implementation and acknowledge they need to upgrade their delivery capabilities. At least 59 per cent of respondents to the most recent EIU survey acknowledge a gap between their strategy design and implementation and recognize its negative impact on organizational effectiveness. That's barely an improvement over the 2013 EIU survey, when 61 per cent of respondents admitted to performance-sapping shortfalls in implementation.

There is, however, no single true path to implementation excellence. Because there are several frameworks for strategy design and implementation, every organization needs to craft its own recipe for strategic success. We believe this recipe will be more effective when it adheres to a set of core principles.

Why are principles are so Important?

At the Brightline Initiative, a coalition of leading global organizations, we have crafted a set of guiding principles to help leaders close the expensive and unproductive gap between strategy design and delivery.

We use the word "principles" for a reason. The Cambridge Dictionary says that a principle can be either a "moral rule" that defines "good behaviour or fair dealing" or a "basic truth" that "explains or controls how something happens or works." We view these principles as both a moral rule and a basic truth.

Practices can change, business models are disrupted, technology evolves, but principles do not change. They are the soul of strategy design and delivery. No matter the conditions of the organization's environment, no matter how complex and challenging its strategic goals, its principles are permanent. They safely guide leaders and teams toward the right decisions, practices, and processes. They enable organizations to counter the threats to the implementation of strategic initiatives and the realization of strategic goals. And they point the way toward more effective behaviours and attitudes and guide the use of appropriate practices, tools, and techniques aligned with the business's needs and challenges.

How we identified the 10 principles

The process of identifying and crafting the 10 principles started in May 2017, when a group of experts, practitioners, and researchers, supported by the Brightline team, met to discuss the most complex challenges that organizations face regarding strategy design and delivery. Some of those challenges are well known, such as the absence of alignment between senior and middle managers on one hand and those responsible for executing the strategy on the other.

Other problems still require further exploration and understanding. How, for example, can people be highly motivated to deliver certain strategic initiatives? And how can organizations deal with failure when they need to deliver results quickly and effectively at all times, with little room for mistakes?

Even without full answers to those and other questions, we were able after that first meeting to initiate a process that melded a scientific approach with the experience and knowledge of leading organizations and experts in the strategy discipline. Intensive discussions and group work produced some very rich content. We then analyzed the results using text mining techniques and cluster analysis to identify key areas for further exploration and refinement. We analyzed the most recent scientific studies and empirical surveys of strategy design and implementation with the aim of corroborating and complementing the ideas and concepts identified in this process.

The outcome of this process was a preliminary set of concepts that evolved into the first version of the principles. We then took the draft principles through several iterations to refine the concepts that underlie the ten Brightline Principles. Our aim was to develop simple, clear, robust, and practical guidance to help leaders succeed at bridging the gap between strategy design and delivery. The members of the Brightline coalition believe that every leader can rely on these ten principles to help them close the gap between strategy design and delivery.

The Brightline Initiative Guiding Principles

1: Acknowledge that strategy delivery is just as important as strategy design.

Strategy delivery doesn't just happen automatically once it is designed! The importance of active and visible leadership cannot be overstated. You invest substantial resources, creative time, and energy in designing the right strategy. You need to give equal priority and attention to delivering it – before you move on to something else. It's an essential part of your role to ensure that your organization has the programme delivery capability it needs to implement your strategy.

2: Accept that you're accountable for delivering the strategy you designed.

Do not underestimate entropy! The orchestration required to succeed in today's fast-changing and complex business environment is enormous. Once you have defined and clearly communicated the strategy, your responsibility shifts to

1: Acknowledge that strategy delivery is just as important as strategy design

2: Accept that you're accountable for delivering the strategy you designed

overseeing the progress of implementation so that the strategy delivers results and achieves its goals. You need to know where in your organization change happens and who manages the programmes that drive that change. You are accountable for proactively addressing emerging gaps and challenges that may impact delivery. Without this discipline, rigor, and care, your strategy has little chance of success.

3: Dedicate and mobilize the right resources.

Inspire and assign the right people to get the job done! Actively balance "running the business" and "changing the business" by selecting and securing the right resources for each – they often have different needs. Recognize that team leadership skills are at a premium, and assign the best leaders with sufficient capacity to tackle head-on the most challenging programmes and those essential for successful strategy implementation.

4: Leverage insight on customers and competitors.

Don't forget to look outside! Continue to monitor customer needs, collect competitor insight, and monitor the market landscape for major risks, unknowns, and dependencies. Advantage in the market flows to those who excel at gaining new insights from an ever-changing business environment and quickly responding with the right decisions and adjustments to both strategy design and delivery.

5: Be bold, stay focused and keep it as simple as possible.

Encourage smart simplicity! Initiating or rapidly reacting to dramatic changes in the business environment is an increasingly important capability for success. Many of the delivery challenges you will face will be complex and interdependent. In the face of this, the best way to remain nimble is to surround yourself with simplifiers rather than complicators. You need people who can get to the core of an opportunity or threat, understand the drivers, deliver the information, and take the action you need in the way you need it. That way, you minimize bureaucracy, explore ideas, take appropriate risks, prioritize work, ensure accountability, and focus on delivering value through your strategic initiatives.

6: Promote team engagement and effective cross-business cooperation.

Beware of the "frozen middle"! Gain genuine buy-in from middle and line managers by engaging and activating them as strategy champions rather than just

3: Dedicate and mobilize the right resources

4: Leverage insight on customers and competitors

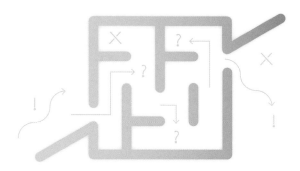

5: Be bold, stay focused and keep it as simple as possible

6: Promote team engagement and effective cross-business cooperation

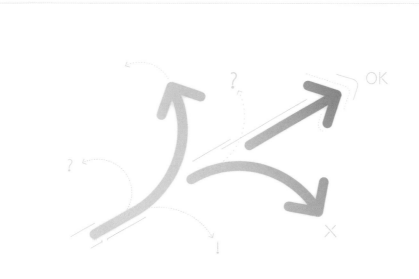

7: Demonstrate bias toward decision-making and own the decisions you make

8: Check ongoing initiatives before committing to new ones

as managers and supervisors. Don't just assume your people will "get it" – leadership must firmly establish a shared commitment to strategy-delivery priorities and regularly reinforce it. This isn't the time or place for subtlety. Govern through transparency to engender trust and enhance cross-business cooperation in delivery.

7: Demonstrate bias toward decision-making and own the decisions you make.

Follow your decisions through to delivery! Commit to making strategic decisions rapidly. Move quickly to correct course, reprioritize, and remove roadblocks. Accept that you likely won't have all the information you want, and rely on those you can trust to deliver sufficient reliable input to allow thoughtful decisions. Consider and address risks and interdependencies explicitly—both upfront and regularly throughout delivery. Build a lean and powerful governance structure to reinforce accountability, ownership, and a bias towards action, based on agreed metrics and milestones.

8: Check ongoing initiatives before committing to new ones.

Resist the temptation to declare victory too soon! With the right governance, leadership, rigor, and reporting capabilities in place, you can regularly evaluate your portfolio of strategic initiatives. Add new initiatives in response to new opportunities, but first be sure you understand both the existing portfolio and your organization's capacity to deliver change. Actively address any issues you discover. In the long term, strategic initiative management discipline – critical for effective orchestration of a dynamic initiative portfolio – will work only if robust assessment, support, and course correction are in place.

9: Develop robust plans but allow for missteps – fail fast to learn fast.

Proper planning and preparation prevent poor performance! The old axiom is as true as it ever was, but in today's business environment, strategy planning cycles must be more rapid, dynamic, and agile than in the past. Empower programme delivery teams to experiment and learn in an environment where it is safe to fail fast. Discuss challenges openly, and adjust the plan as needed for success. Learn to reward failure, or at least accept it as valuable input.

10: Celebrate success and recognize those who have done good work.

Inspiring people is part of your job! Yes, you have to drive accountability and focus on delivery, but you also need to motivate those who do the work. Actively

9: Develop robust plans but allow for missteps – fail fast to learn fast

10: Celebrate success and recognize those who have done good work

shape a winning culture by engaging and exciting the people responsible for delivering strategic change programmes. Celebrate successes and quick wins. Generously and publicly acknowledge those who demonstrate the leadership behaviours and programme delivery capabilities that make strategy succeed, and ask them to share their experiences.

Organizations rise or fall on their ability to successfully implement winning strategies. At a time when leaders are expected to do nothing less than transform their organizations so that they can survive and prosper in a hyper-connected, fast-changing world, they urgently need to know how to turn ideas into reality. We at the Brightline Initiative are ready, willing, and eager to help leaders and their organizations build their implementation capabilities. We offer these 10 principles as a first step on a long and, we hope, ultimately rewarding journey toward implementation excellence.

About the authors

 Ricardo Viana Vargas is Executive Director of the Brightline Initiative (brightline.org).

 Edivandro Conforto is Strategy Research Advisor for the Brightline Initiative (brightline.org).

Resources

Economist Intelligence Unit (EIU), "Closing the Gap: Designing and Delivering a Strategy that Works", 2017.

Economist Intelligence Unit (EIU), "Why good strategies fail: Lessons from the C-suite" 2013.

Project Management Institute (PMI), "PMI's Pulse of the Profession: Success Rates Rise – Transforming the high cost of low performance", 9th Global Project Management Survey, 2017.

'THE WORLD ISN'T STATIC. STRATEGY ISN'T STATIC, BUT THAT DOESN'T MEAN THERE ISN'T A WAY OF THINKING ABOUT THE FUNDAMENTAL QUESTIONS IN A WAY THAT KEEPS YOU AHEAD OF THE COMPETITION.'

ROGER MARTIN

ALEX OSTERWALDER & YVES PIGNEUR

The business portfolio map

We have prototyped a new tool called the Business Portfolio Map. The aim: to help organizations understand if the business is prepared for the future or risks disruption.

The Business Portfolio Map visualizes a company's entire portfolio of business models on a single map. In the image above you can see the full concept which is composed of the execution engine (exploit/improve) and the innovation engine (explore/invent). The Business Portfolio Map visualises all of your existing businesses, as well as all of your new growth initiatives. This holistic view shows you if your company is prone to disruption, at risk, or if you are prepared for the future. More importantly, the Business Portfolio Map can help companies make better investment decisions.

Let's walk through how the Business Portfolio Map works.

The Execution Engine: Exploit/Improve

This is where you manage your existing businesses. In your business portfolio, you hope to keep all your businesses highly profitable and sustainable at the top right of the exploit Map. In our prototype, Yves and I visualize the portfolio of existing businesses on two axis:

1. Profitability: How much profit do the existing business models generate? Business models with high profit margins, and a lot of profit, sit at the top end of the spectrum. Low profit margins and low profit overall sit at the bottom – these could potentially be very large businesses but they are not very profitable. This of course is the most traditional end of the spectrum.

2. Sustainability or disruption risk: How sustainable is your business model, and how likely is it to be disrupted? Models at risk may be very established businesses, but prone to disruption for technology, market, or regulatory changes. Those companies sit on the left hand side. Strong business models with moats to protect them on the other hand are very unlikely to be disrupted. They sit on the right hand side.

Businesses that fall from the top right down to the left are dying or sick businesses that you need to take care of. It may not necessarily mean you kill

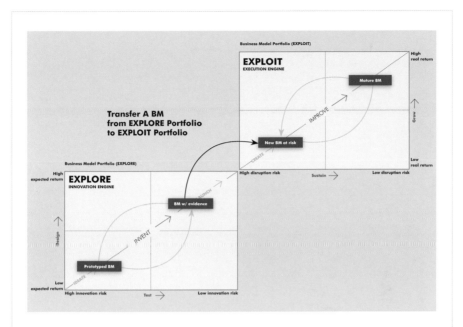

Explore and Exploit BM Portfolios

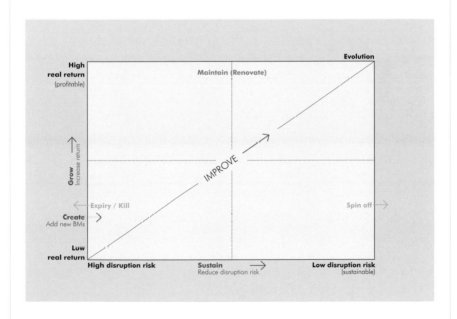

Business Model Portfolio (Exploit)

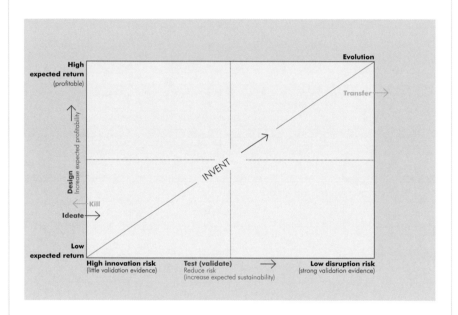

Business Model Portfolio (Explore)

those businesses – that may be an option, but ultimately it's about renovating, improving and sometimes reinventing the business and moving it up to the top right hand corner.

New businesses that graduate from the Innovation Engine to the Execution Engine usually start out at the bottom left. They are still very fragile, barely profitable, and need a lot of care. Your goal is also to move them up to the top right hand corner.

Ultimately, a healthy Execution Portfolio has a good number of businesses at the top right, a number of young new businesses at the bottom left, and as few as possible anywhere else.

The Innovation Engine: Explore/Invent

When it comes to the Innovation Engine, you want to explore many, many different ideas. New business models and initiatives will start out at the bottom left of the map: their profit potential is unclear and you have little evidence to prove that the idea is likely to work. You have to iteratively design, test, and adapt the idea, its value propositions, and business models until it makes it to the top right hand corner: a tested business idea with substantial profit potential.

To visualize the portfolio of potential new businesses we use two axis, similar to the business model portfolio of existing businesses:

1. Expected return: Ideas and initiatives that have only limited potential to create substantial future revenues and profits go at the bottom of the spectrum. Limitations include size of market, revenue potential, pricing, etc.. Business models with large potential revenues and profits sit at the top of the spectrum. Equally important here is to judge how robust a business model is: e.g. in terms of recurring revenues, long term growth, scalability, protection from competition, etc.

2. Innovation risk: On this axis you evaluate how much you de-risked a good looking business initiative. Ideas for which you have no evidence yet are very risky to invest in--these new initiatives sit on the left hand side. Ideas for which you rigorously test desirability, viability, and feasibility sit on the right hand side of the spectrum. The more you are confident an initiative will work based on tests and the resulting evidence, the more they move to the right. The more they are on the right hand side, the less risky they are to invest in.

The particularity of the Innovation Engine is that you need a lot of cheap projects at the bottom left in order to product a winner that makes it to the top right. You need to explore, prototype, and test many ideas cheaply and quickly to learn and adapt. The investment at this stage isn't big. The more evidence you gather that an idea might work, the more you invest and start to move the idea up towards the right. Out of ten ideas maybe five will die, three will remain mediocre, and two will be home runs.

Be careful not to push promising ideas from the Innovation Engine into the execution space too quickly. These young businesses need traction, stability, and protection when you move them into the execution engine. They might get swallowed up by the execution engine or killed by the dominant business models' antibodies – it's a corporate habit that can kill your innovation engine.

Are you prepared for the future?

The Business Portfolio Map visualizes how prepared your organization is for the future. You have an obvious challenge if you have only a few businesses at the top right in the execution engine, and a lot of business at risk with low returns. You have an even bigger challenge when your innovation engine shows few new promising and validated future growth engines in the pipeline.

The ultimate goal of a balanced Business Portfolio Map is to show good, solid business models at the top right, and a lot of fresh new ideas at the bottom left. A few of those ideas should be creeping up to the top right of the explore square and soon make it to the Execution Engine. If you can visualize that for your business then you can say you're prepared for the future.

Amazon is an example we frequently cite of a company that intentionally manages a diverse portfolio of existing and promising new business models. The company continues to produce growth with its existing businesses (e-commerce, AWS, logistics, etc.), while juggling a portfolio of potential future growth engines that may become big profit generators one day (e.g. Alexa, Echo, Dash Button, Prime Air, Amazon Fresh, Mayday Button, etc.).

How can you manage your business model portfolio?

We put together three steps to get started with the Business Portfolio Map:

1. Assess: Evaluate your present business model portfolio by analysing current and future business contribution (profitability & potential of new ideas) and risk (disruption risk & validation of new ideas).

2. Strategize: Define objectives, allocate resources and design your desired future business model portfolio. In other words, define actions in the Execution Engine (increasing returns / reducing disruption risk) and the Innovation Engine (allocating resources for new ideas and testing).

3. Process: Implement your innovation strategy and transform your portfolio with three type of actions:

1. Create: acquire or transfer businesses from the innovation engine.
2. Raise: Move businesses from the bottom left towards the top right corner.
3. Eliminate: Sometimes businesses can be divested or spun off.

'THE COMMON QUESTION THAT GETS ASKED IN BUSINESS IS "WHY?" THAT'S A GOOD QUESTION, BUT AN EQUALLY VALID ONE IS "WHY NOT?"

JEFF BEZOS

STUART CRAINER & DES DEARLOVE

Only communicate

Imagine you are a CEO. You take your top team away for a strategy session at a suitably well-furnished hotel somewhere in the countryside. Over two days of discussions, you emerge with a great new strategy for the organization. The future is mapped out with brilliant simplicity, markets will be disrupted, the competition won't know what has hit them. You get back to the office and let some bright consultants loose to test out the strategy. The numbers add up, the insights into where the market is going appear robust, and then… Well, and then you put the brilliantly conceived strategy into the top drawer of your desk (next to the hip flask, picture of your first love and ancient teddy bear).

Sound far-fetched? Of course, if you don't tell anyone about your strategy it is unlikely to become reality. How can you galvanize people if they don't actually know what the strategy is?

Yet, this is what happens repeatedly in organizations. The creation of strategy is something which business schools, consultants, coaches and advisors have mastered. In contrast, actually communicating the strategy to the world is something which tends to be left to minions or to forces of nature. CEOs don't put the strategy documents into a drawer and then forget about them, but sometimes they might as well have done.

In many organizations fundamental questions remain hanging in the air mysteriously. What is a company's mission? And what is its strategy to win in the market? Basic questions, but ones which often go unanswered by some of the world's leading corporations.

Research by ECSI Consulting (ecsi-consulting.com) looked at the top 50 companies in the Fortune 500 ranking of US companies. It examined how the companies communicated their mission and strategies in their annual reports and websites.

The research found that vagueness, inconsistency and elusiveness are the reality – worrying news for any investors seeking to find out more about a company before investing or for potential employees of these corporate giants trying to learn more about the companies.

"The results are disturbing for investors, employees and many others," says

Alessandro Di Fiore of ECSI (who we featured on the Thinkers50 Radar for 2016). "How can companies and their leaders be held to account if their purpose and the strategies they are seeking to execute are not clearly and consistently communicated?"

While 94 per cent included their mission statement on their website, only half of the companies included their mission statement in their annual report.

Strategies are similarly difficult to pin down, i.e. a clear statement on how the company is going to win in the market and gain clients. A total of 58 per cent of the companies included their strategy in their annual report. But only a mere 12 per cent included a dedicated, clearly articulated strategy section. On websites, 54 per cent included some kind of strategy description.

Strangely perhaps, the most elusive sector is the high-tech world of computing, ICT and telecoms. Here companies appear unwilling to be bound by static guidelines or held hostage by public statements of strategy. Perhaps the logic is that the tech world is moving so quickly that any notion of strategy is likely to be proved worthless, better to be opportunistically vague about your intent.

But it's not only the fact that information is notable by its absence. When companies do share details of their missions and strategies, the results are often underwhelming.

The obvious is often re-stated with buzzwords added to suggest industry know-how. Goals, such as "creating competitive advantage" or "being innovative", are routinely mistaken for strategy. And there is a repetitive focus on "maximizing shareholder value", "delivering profitable growth" and so on.

"A good strategy description should answer three fundamental questions," says Alessandro di Fiore. "How are we going to win in the market? How we are different? And why is that difference relevant for our existing and potential customers?"

But vagueness rules in many annual reports. Strategy statements are usually unable to answer the question: "How is the company going to win in the market and attract customers?" The insurance giant AIG, for example, states: "Our strategy is focused on enhancing the value and competitive position of our insurance businesses and investing our capital where we can achieve attractive risk-adjusted returns, while maintaining strong levels of liquidity and capital."

Others make elusiveness their strategy. Apple is notably reticent while Walgreens, the drug store chain, chooses to brazen it out with the simple statement: "We do not provide detailed information on specific topics, such as our corporate strategy."

Some companies do meet the strategic clarity challenge. "Our strategy is to provide our members with a broad range of high quality merchandise at prices consistently lower than they can obtain elsewhere," says Costco while Microsoft says its strategy is to "build best-in-class platforms and productivity services for a mobile-first, cloud-first world".

"A strategy should be able to be distilled down to 15 compelling, meaningful and memorable words articulating how we are going to win in the marketplace," says Alessandro di Fiore. "It needs then to be communicated clearly and consistently inside and outside. This research suggests there is still a long way to go for this to be achieved. Even on the most fundamental company's document for all stakeholders – the Annual Report – there are gaps".

You might say that annual reports and website information is for the external world and that companies may well be communicating their strategies brilliantly internally. This may be so in some organizations, but it seems unlikely. Vagueness and obfuscation are habitual and cultural. Where would you like to work? Where would you choose to invest your money? In a company which clearly and repeatedly articulates its mission and strategy or one which does not?

There is little doubt that communication issues are set to become ever more important as information becomes ever more pervasive and instantly communicated. There is no place to hide.

Talking with Columbia Business School's Rita McGrath, this is what she observed: "The difference in leadership behaviour that you're going to be seeing is an emphasis much more on information travelling fast. So I use the example of Ford and Alan Mulally, when he was CEO at Ford, who basically said, you can't manage a secret. So we're going to see a lot less of the management of, bring me the numbers, hit the goals, don't bring me bad news, don't bring me a problem that you don't have a solution to. That kind of management, which works really well when things are stable, we're going to see that going away.

"We're going to see a lot more leadership that involves influencing people and getting people engaged. We're going to see much more candour, much more emphasis on being realistic and also much more emphasis on keeping individuals and networks engaged, because in the past you used to be able to say a hierarchical reward was going to be the thing, so you start off at level 14 and you end up at level two and that's Nirvana. I think we will see much less of that in how we manage careers in the future or how leaders engage people in the future." The twenty-first century is a time of transparent, instant communication – and that applies to your organization's strategy.

'IN ACTION, BE PRIMITIVE; IN FORESIGHT, A STRATEGIST.'

RENÉ CHAR

ESSENTIAL THINKER

Richard D'Aveni

Few thinkers manage to change the vocabulary of their area of study and then influence it for decades. Richard D'Aveni has done just that in the sphere of strategy. His career has roamed as widely as his ever-curious intellect.

The starting point for D'Aveni was the book, *Hypercompetition*, which established the term in the strategic vocabulary and became a highly influential bestseller.

Since then he has set about reinventing strategy with a focus on using rapid maneuvering rather than defensive barriers. More Sun-Tzu than Michael Porter, D'Aveni advocates temporary advantages and the constant disruption of rivals.

His books focus on creating new tools, frameworks and maps that help firms and governments define their playing fields and determine their positioning using spheres of influence. They include *Strategic Supremacy* and *Beating the Commodity Trap*.

D'Aveni has gone on to apply his concepts to the very notion of capitalism and what he sees as the hypercompetition, which now exists between nations. These ideas are captured in his book *Strategic Capitalism*.

Most recently, in a series of influential articles, D'Aveni has charted the rise of 3-D printing and its likely impact on the world of manufacturing.

A professor of strategy at the Tuck School of Business at Dartmouth College, Richard D'Aveni works with *Fortune 500* companies as well as governments and some of the world's wealthiest families. His classes are notable for the involvement of some of America's leading CEOs.

Richard D'Aveni

Face-to-face, Richard D'Aveni is a big man, with incisively large opinions; keen to tackle the big ideas. We asked him about the genesis of *Hypercompetition*:

The book came about because of a very strange event. I went to Cape Cod in Massachusetts for a vacation, and a hurricane came along called Hurricane Bob. While I was there it knocked out all the electricity for about four days. When the electricity came back on CNN was running a programme on the fall of the Soviet Union. I had no idea that something like that could happen in a few days. It was one of the most important, economic, and political changes of our generation.

So I stepped back and said to myself, I'm teaching all of these students about long-term plans and consistent strategies, how do you really do that in a world where significant earth shattering changes appear overnight? How do you do that when, even if you had all the resources of the Central Intelligence Agency, you still couldn't figure out that it was going to happen? I thought to myself, I must be a fraud, and decided to sit down and write a book that was about unsustainable advantages in an unpredictable world, rather than the traditional view of strategy.

So you described the world we're now in?

Yes, that's right. Except I think the world has become even crazier since 1994, it's really hypercompetition on steroids today. It's even more relevant today than it was when I first wrote it. The core idea was that advantages were becoming unsustainable because of globalization and technological disruption. Globalization is accelerating because of the rise of China and India, and the falling entry barriers around numerous other countries. Of course, technology hasn't slowed down at all; it's expanding. The Internet, which was once considered to be revolutionary, is now par for the course everywhere, still having the same radicalization effect on many, many markets. Just we don't talk about it anymore, because it's so endemic in every marketplace.

In such a disorderly, chaotic world, isn't strategy and more wishful thinking than a constructive use of an executive style?

Yes, that's the whole point of hypercompetition. What I argued was that long-term strategies, strategies about sequencing, lots of short-term advantages and exploring your way forward, the way Lewis and Clark found the Northwest Passage to the Pacific is what you have to do. You only know what direction you're headed in when you go from hilltop to hilltop looking around for the next hilltop. You can't chart the course all the way from beginning to end, the way you might have been able to 20 years ago when things were stable. You can't know where you're going to end up in this kind of world, and you have to be used to the uncertainty, you have to have tolerance for that kind of a world, but have the faith and the courage to be able to move forward from hilltop to hilltop and not get caught in the intellectual trap of thinking that you have to continue to leverage the same competence that you had one year ago or five years ago, because it won't get you to where you're going.

RICHARD D'AVENI

In praise of additives

In the late 1980s, Motorola faced a major threat to its fast-growing cell phone business. Rivals were developing digital technology to replace the existing analog standard. Internal debate raged. Should Motorola keep its focus on analog, or switch over to digital? Build off its core competence, or play from weakness? Could both technologies exist side by side? Or would only one survive?

Engineers at the company came down squarely on the side of analog. Digital, they pointed out, was simply inferior to analog as a medium for storing and transmitting audio. After all, it stripped away 60 per cent of the information contained in the original analog message.

What those engineers couldn't see was that, for most listeners, digital technology's advantages far outweighed the often undetectable losses from digitization. That's partly because they had spent much of their lives building up their expertise in analog technology. A shift to digital would require them to learn a great deal from scratch. So it was easier to see the negatives than the positives. The end result was that Motorola's conversion to digital took much longer than it needed to. The company lost its leadership of the very industry that it had invented back in 1973. And it wasn't alone – another audio leader, Sony, similarly lost market share in electronics because of its analog bias.

An equivalent challenge is now looming for companies in many industries. 3D printing, or "additive manufacturing," essentially digitizes the production process. Like digital audio in the 1980s, this young technology has some drawbacks compared to conventional "subtractive" manufacturing. But as I explained in a *Harvard Business Review* article, the flexibility and versatility it offers will eventually make it the preferred choice for companies in many industries. And the opportunities to combine parts, reduce inventory costs, and earn a premium price for customization often compensate for the higher direct costs of 3D printing.

I recently attended a private conference with panels led by manufacturing experts from multi-billion dollar firms. One after another they explained why 3D printing wasn't ready for high-volume manufacturing in their industry. They feared problems with durability and strength, not to mention customer reactions to the horror of discovering that their products were printed. (It was as though they'd never heard of Walmart, whose profitability depended on selling products from overseas factories with lower quality standards.)

Then a young woman shook things up. She got up to the podium and said, "It's a good thing I never met any of you before. Otherwise my firm wouldn't have made $40 million last year. You are so busy looking at what 3D printing can't do that you're ignoring what it can do!"

While her competitors had dismissed additive manufacturing because it couldn't (at that point) print an entire product, she had focused on just one element of the product. Her firm ramped up from 100 customized parts to 10,000 in just one year. It is now expanding into other parts, and will soon be able to offer customization of the overall product at a premium price. As the company moves down the learning curve and costs come down, the savings from reduced waste, inventory, and assembly labor will even make it competitive for the mass production segment of the market.

Her secret is a process I call "Just Say Yes": Listen to what your engineers say, then put them to work solving those problems one by one, even if the solutions aren't immediately apparent. Just say yes is much like Gene Krantz's famous command, "Failure is not an option," when faced with the Apollo 13 crisis that nearly killed three astronauts on the way to the moon. Here's the process in four steps:

1. Gather knowledge from the outside. Don't rely solely on your in-house engineers – some of them are likely to be guardians of the status quo. Reach out to additive manufacturing printer and software providers, and your industry associations, to see what already exists for your product categories. Talk to universities and governmental laboratories to learn about the current state of 3D printing and how well it performs on the materials and attributes that your customers prefer   not just the ones you have always provided. Include your staff engineers on the learning teams but make sure they don't dominate the discussion.

2. Move one baby step at time. Build expertise and reduce internal resistance through incremental experiments, exploring and adjusting to new technological development as you go. Engineers love challenges, so internally you can set up tiny, non-threatening pilot programmes and see where these take you. Always listen to skeptics and take the problems seriously, but project confidence that the kinks will be worked out over time.

3. Focus and prioritize. No firm can explore the many possibilities of additive manufacturing all at once. So you'll want to start with the most promising and feasible choices first, and build up small wins. But don't expect a carefully planned sequence of development. As technology and the industry ecosystems develop, you may well adjust your priorities as you meet various milestones.

4. Keep an eye on the long run. Especially for large companies, the goal is to revamp the industry's value chain and ecosystem to reduce total costs of the value chain and especially your firm. So look for opportunities to develop or support an emerging software platform or superior printer technology. Your explorations should have a logical, cohesive, long-term goal of pulling together the initiatives into an integrated 3D-printing-based manufacturing system.

With enough encouragement, you'll see 3D printing champions emerge in your organization to help drive the process forward and build momentum. Some people (and organizations) won't be able to embrace the technology in time and will be passed by. If you keep Motorola and Sony in mind, you won't be one of them.

About the author

 Richard D'Aveni is the Bakala Professor of Strategy at Dartmouth College's Tuck School of Business.

This blog was originally published online by *Harvard Business Review*.

'DO IT, FIX IT, TRY IT.'

TOM PETERS & ROBERT WATERMAN

ALESSANDRO DI FIORE

The power of judgement

What marks the great business leaders apart is not their capacity for hard work. Virtually all work insanely long hours. Nor is it their intelligence. Most CEOs are smart people. Nor is it good fortune. In life and business luck tends to even out over a life or a career.

No, what separates the great from the merely good is the ability to make judgements. Great leaders have the capacity to speedily and decisively reach conclusions and act upon them.

Think of Steve Jobs. When he returned to Apple it was a mess. The emphasis had been on developing more and more products. Apple was selling printers in partnership with Hewlett Packard and making next to no money on them. Focus had been lost and managers were increasingly addicted to elaborate PowerPoint presentations. Jobs cut the numbers of models and products. He drew a simple two-by-two diagram and said the company needed a product in each quadrant. He banned PowerPoint. When he discovered the realities of the partnership with HP, Jobs left the meeting and called the head of HP to cancel the arrangement.

Steve Jobs was highly resistant to quantitative research. Apple was built on insights rather than analytics.

The capability to generate and apply insights and qualitative judgments to innovation is a key competitive advantage – or, at least, should be.

The trouble is that most companies use a number-driven approach to innovation. Companies invest heavily in developing analytical skills. In recent years, investments have poured into analytics and big data to increase organizational analytical power. Innovation processes have been re-engineered, or over-engineered, with stage-gate processes equipped with financial evaluation tools to support the go/no go decisions and the release of resources at each stage. In their search for numbers, analysts look for benchmarks, from which they can extrapolate impressive-looking business cases and forecasts. Before you know it, the decision has been taken and the company committed to a me-too innovation.

The result is that qualitative perceptions don't get an airing. Strategy and innovation should not be a mere exercise of analytical power, but a qualitative process in which the analysis serves insights born out of individual observation and reflection, rather than the other way round.

Why do business leaders struggle so much in incorporating qualitative judgment into their innovation decisions? Our research uncovered two main causes.

First, is what can be called Schumpeter's bias, after the famous economist Joseph Schumpeter theory of creative destruction. We all pay lip service to Schumpeter's vision of the lone and creative entrepreneur. This image is so entrenched that people unconsciously tend to believe that the magic of an insight is not replicable. Many business leaders believe that we depend on "individual" genetic talent. But scientific evidence of the last 30 years proves just the opposite.

A famous study on identical twins aged between 15 and 22 years found that while 80 per cent of IQ differences were attributable to genetics, only around 30 per cent of the performance on creativity tests could be explained that way. Many of the traits we assume to be genetically determined are in fact the product of one's environment. That's a tremendously significant finding in support of the idea that we can work on learning and improving our creativity.

Of course, not every child will be a Leonardo da Vinci, nor will every young manager be a Steve Jobs. But people who point to that fact are missing the one really important truth about creativity: there's two types of creativity. Creativity as in genius (the big C) and creativity as in attitude, thinking ability and mindset (the little c). We tend to muddle these two quite different sorts of creativity.

For example, if you dig into the back-story of Apple, you'll soon realize that it wasn't all about Steve Jobs. He was actually wrong a lot of the time. If it had been entirely up to him, Apple would have never opened the App Store. What made Apple great was the combination of Jobs' genius with the little c of the people he worked with and who weren't afraid to express their own ideas. Jobs understood that as well — not, perhaps, in his first spell at the company, but certainly in his second. When asked what he thought was his most important creation, rather than mentioning the iPod or iPhone, Jobs said it was Apple, the company. He claimed that "making an enduring company was both harder and more important than making a great product."

Arguably, little c creativity is more critical in business than big C.

The second element at work is discomfort with qualitative judgments. Measuring is comforting. Companies, mostly large ones, need to maintain some kind of control over processes, and playing the management-by-numbers-game makes decision makers feel more confident. Moreover, the act of measurement is generally seen as a guarantee of unbiased results. Enraptured by the Holy Grail of quantitative analysis, business leaders are so obsessed by numbers that they rarely question their guidance. Preoccupied with issues such as predictability and control, they have become increasingly suspicious of qualitative perceptions.

However comforting it might be to stick with what you can measure, leadership isn't about feeling comfortable. It's about catching opportunities as they occur, even when the numbers suggest otherwise.

Consider the story of Nespresso by Nestlè, which has become Europe's leading brand of premium-portioned coffee. Nespresso machines brew espresso from coffee aluminum capsules, a type of pre-apportioned single-use container of various high-quality coffees and flavourings. The Nespresso brand took off when it stopped targeting offices and started marketing itself to households. Behavioural evidence on how households would respond to the new concept was poor and suggested that consumers' intentions to purchase did not meet quantitative threshold requirements set by market research protocols at Nestlè. Jean-Paul Gaillard, a young marketing head of Nespresso at the time, believed strongly in the product and thanks to his skillful interpretation of the data convinced the company to take the risk. If he had only listened to quantitative research, the concept would have never got off the ground.

Analysis is useful. No question. But, the reality is that judgement is the driving power behind innovation.

About the author

 Alessandro Di Fiore is the founder and CEO of the European Centre for Strategic Innovation (www.ecsi-consulting.com) and chairman of *Harvard Business Review Italia*.

'TRY NOT. DO, OR DO NOT. THERE IS NO TRY.'

YODA

ZHANG RUIMIN

Why enterprises exist

The fundamental purpose of enterprises is not to make money.

What then is the fundamental purpose of an enterprise? It is to create users. Imagine a two-dimensional graph, with a vertical and a horizontal axis. The horizontal axis is substantially the same as other general businesses, we call it 'enterprise value' – the market goal is, in short, to create customers. Customers and users are not the same thing, and should be separated. 'Customers' make a one time transaction with the enterprise: you make a product, the customer buys it, you hand it over, and there is no further contact. 'Users', on the other hand, interact with you, are brand loyal and give their opinions, so you can continue to improve. So, the horizontal axis is customers, and the vertical axis is users, we call it the 'value of network'. The vertical axis fully shows how you are creating users. In the Internet era, this is through interaction with users.

We have changed the perspective. In the past I would ask about our market share. I would ask how many tens of thousands of products we had sold and whether the market share had reached 20 per cent. But things are different now. We are concerned about whether those 20 per cent of users are interacting with us. If there is no interaction, then this is only a customer and not a user in the real sense. We used to say that making money was the end of the sales process, but now that is the start of a new sales process. In the past, users were just purchasers, whereas now users have become participants.

In the past there may not have been any interaction, but there was a kind of gaming. This so-called gaming could apply to suppliers, for example, mainly around the price, meaning we would use whatever was cheapest. While, the relationship with the user is more like a marketing game, where the question is how we can use promotional materials to make you believe in our products. Because of information asymmetry, whoever communicates most is more likely to get the user's favour. For employees, the game may be about getting more control, how to strengthen the enterprise development by controlling employees. So, we first need to change our conception, changing from gaming to interaction, and we want interaction in every aspect to add value.

About the author

 Zhang Ruimin is CEO of the Haier Group (haier.net).

This is an edited extract from *Haier Purpose* by Hu Yong and Hao Yazhou (Thinkers50 and Infinite ideas, 2017).

'COMPANIES DON'T PRODUCE STRATEGIES, JUST PLANS.'

GARY HAMEL

ALISON REYNOLDS & DAVID LEWIS

The difference that makes a difference

Looking around the executive teams we work with as consultants and those we teach in the classroom, increased diversity of gender, ethnicity, and age is apparent. Over recent decades the rightful endeavour to achieve a more representative workforce has had an impact. Of course, there is a way to go but progress has been made.

Throughout this period, we have run a strategic execution exercise with executive groups focused on managing new, uncertain and complex situations. The exercise requires the group to formulate and execute a strategy to achieve a specified outcome, against the clock.

Received wisdom is that the more diverse the teams (in terms of age, ethnicity, and gender), the more creative and productive they are likely to be. But, in our exercise some groups fared exceptionally well and others incredibly badly, regardless of their apparent diversity. This was corroborated when we looked at the data; we found no correlation between successful outcomes in the execution of the exercise and diversity in the executive teams.

When there is so much focus on the importance of diversity in problem solving we were intrigued by these results. If not diversity, then what accounted for such variability in performance? We wanted to understand what led some groups to succeed and others to crash and burn. This led us to consider differences that go beyond gender, ethnicity or age. Differences referred to under the heading of cognitive diversity.

Cognitive diversity has been defined as differences in perspective or information processing styles. It is not predicted by factors such as gender, ethnicity or age. Here we are interested in a specific aspect of cognitive diversity, how individuals think about and engage with new, uncertain and complex situations. We call this kind of cognitive diversity 'thinkversity'.

The AEM Cube®, a tool developed by Peter Roberson, a psychiatrist and business consultant, assesses differences in the way people approach change. It measures:

- Knowledge processing: The extent to which individuals prefer to consolidate and deploy existing knowledge, or prefer to generate new knowledge, when facing new situations

- Perspective: The extent to which individuals prefer to deploy their own expertise, or prefer to orchestrate the ideas and expertise of others, when facing new situations

We used this tool to measure the different levels of thinkversity in teams undertaking the strategic execution exercise. Our analysis across six teams who undertook the exercise shows a significant correlation between high thinkversity and high performance in the exercise.

Intuitively this makes sense. Tackling new challenges requires a balance between applying what we know and discovering what we don't know that might be useful. It also requires individual application of specialized expertise and the ability to step back and look at the bigger picture.

A high degree of thinkversity generates accelerated learning and performance in the face of new uncertain and complex situations, as in the case of the execution problem we set for our executives. These cognitive preferences are established when we are young. They are independent of our education, our culture and other social conditioning. Two things about thinkversity make it particularly easy to overlook:

1. Thinkversity is less visible

First, it is less visible than ethnic and gender diversity, for example.

Being a man or woman, from a different culture or of a different generation, gives no clue as to how that person might process information, engage with or respond to change. We cannot easily detect thinkversity from the outside. It cannot be predicted or easily orchestrated. The very fact that thinkversity is an internal difference requires us to work hard to surface it and harness the benefits.

2. Cultural barriers to thinkversity

The second factor that contributes to thinkversity being overlooked is that we create cultural barriers that restrict the degree of thinkversity, even when we don't mean to.

We are familiar with the saying 'we recruit in our own image', but this bias doesn't end with our formal recruitment processes. We continue to gravitate towards the people who think and express themselves in a similar way to ourselves. As a result, we often end up in like-minded teams. When this happens, we have functional bias and low thinkversity.

Functional bias is a problem for teams facing new uncertain and complex situations because with little thinkversity the ability to see things differently, engage in different ways (e.g. experiment, versus analyzing) and create new options, are limited. Similarly, when organizations initiate change programmes they often seek out and identify 'advocates' or 'change agents' to support activities. Those selected often have a similar approach to change. This lack of thinkversity has two impacts. First, it reduces the opportunity to strengthen the proposition with input from people who think differently. Second, it fails to represent the thinkversity of the employee population reducing the impact of engagement initiatives often spearheaded by change agents.

If you look for it, thinkversity is all around but people like to fit in and are cautious about sticking their necks out. When we have a strong homogenous culture (e.g. an engineering culture, an operational culture, or a relationship culture), we stifle the natural thinkversity in groups through the pressure to conform.

There is much talk of authentic leadership, i.e. being yourself. Perhaps it is even more important that leaders focus on enabling others to be themselves as opposed to homogenised holograms generated from the generic competency frameworks leaders put in place.

Psychological safety

If thinkversity is what we need to succeed in dealing with new, uncertain and complex situations, we need to overcome cultural barriers and encourage people to reveal and deploy their thinkversity. We need to recognize the expression of authentic drives and responses, instincts and preferences; to make it safe to be yourself, to try, to fail and try again. Far more important than to have all the answers, creating psychological safety is the prime responsibility of today's leaders.

Three principles to enhance your thinkversity
- Makes sure your recruitment processes identify difference and recruit for thinkversity
- When facing a new, uncertain complex situation, and everyone agrees on what to do, find someone who disagrees and cherish them
- Focus on creating a psychologically safe environment where everyone, including the leader, can openly contribute their perspectives, experiences and vulnerabilities wholeheartedly.

About the authors

Alison Reynolds (alison.reynolds@ashridge.hult.edu) is a member of faculty at the UK's Ashridge Business School where she works with executive groups in the field of leadership development, strategy execution and organization development.

David Lewis (dlewis@london.edu) is Programme Director of London Business School's Senior Executive Programme and teaches on strategy execution and leading in uncertainty. He is co-founder of a research company focusing on developing tools to enhance individual, team and organization performance through better interaction.

'UNHAPPY THE GENERAL WHO COMES ON THE FIELD OF BATTLE WITH A SYSTEM.'

NAPOLEON BONAPARTE

ALF REHN

The real lessons of disruption

Ever since Clayton Christensen introduced the notion of "disruptive innovation" in *The Innovator's Dilemma* (1997), CEOs everywhere have found within themselves a desire to be disruptors. Seeing as it is a logical necessity that only very few can pull this off, one might wonder why this is the case. Why do so many leaders dream of radical overhaul and overthrowing the established order? In part the answer lies in how well the concept has captured the Zeitgeist of our era. In an age which celebrates the new and the innovative – at times to the point of fetishism – it is natural that captains of industry would want to align themselves with the notion of disruption, as not doing so would imply one is about to be disrupted. But what happens in a situation where most if not all strive for disruptive innovation?

And the trouble does not end there. Recently, the concept of disruption has come under increasing attack. In part this has been due to the overuse of the word, leading to a perceived lack of meaning – when everything is portrayed as disruptive, the concept starts sounding like a joke. In part this has been due to a lack of clarity as to what a theory of disruption explains. Jill Lepore attacked Clayton Christensen, highlighting how many of the cases used by the latter didn't seem to say what he claimed they said, and further that Christensen's proposed theory of disruption didn't seem to have strong predictive capacities.

What this shows is that while we've become very comfortable with using the word 'disruption', this hasn't necessarily translated into an understanding of how disruption works, nor what is required to truly be a disruptor. Further, we need to be aware of the fact that disruption is not necessarily a model to be emulated, but rather a lesson to be learned! So, in this spirit, five lessons to embrace:

1. Disruption is an umbrella, not a scalpel. The key reason disruption has become so popular a concept is because it can refer to a great many things, some of them quite dissimilar. While initially used to explain a specific kind of technological disequilibria, it has been used, even by Christensen himself, to describe changes in education, healthcare, or shifts in demographics or geo-political power. This could be seen as proof positive that the term has become devoid of explanatory power, but might also be seen as a kind of meta-validation of the insistence in the original theory that change in a market or industry often emerges from unexpected directions. The lesson theories of disruption might be trying to teach us, then, is that we shouldn't imagine disruption comes in easily discernible guises, or remains the same. Hunting for the next "Uber for X" is then to act against theories of disruption, as this works from the idea that disruption can have a formula. Michel Foucault once said: "Do not ask who I am and do not ask me to remain the same: leave it to our bureaucrats and our police to see that our papers are in order." Something similar might be said of disruption. Once you think you get it, that ain't no longer it – even if you are Clay Christensen.

2. It's not always what you do, but to whom It Is done. A continuation of the point above would be to note that we need to separate the disruption from the disruptive agent. Take, for instance, Uber, one of the contemporary poster-children of disruptive innovation. It has, as a company, been highly disruptive to the entrenched taxi industry, and as its valuation reaches ever more ridiculous heights seems to prove the power inherent in doing so. But what was the disruption, really? On one level, Uber merely leveraged existing technologies – the mobile internet and the notion of a "sharing economy" – in a traditional industry, if with some aplomb. In fact, precious little of what Uber achieved would have been possible had not the existing players (i.e. taxi companies and associated institutions) been so traditional in their outlook and work practices. The lesson we might take away from this, then, is that disruption might not be so much the genius work of the upstart or the startup, but rather something akin to a chemical reaction. Just as a fire cannot start from a spark alone, but requires flammable material to be present, you never disrupt in a vacuum.

3. Think fitness, not war. The discourse on strategy still suffers from a machismo bias, one most easily spotted in the manner it uses terms and metaphors linked to war. But all the talk about "battle-plans" and "the right to win" means less and less in an economy that is permanently changing and churning. A war can be won. A battle too. They have starting shots and final negotiations, and are thus terrible metaphors for modern business.

What disruption can teach us is that there is no endgame, no final victory, for every disruptor will in time be disrupted, and you only win for the most fleeting of moments. A better metaphor, drawn from the notion of disruptive innovation, would be one of fitness. Here, you try to continuously increase your physical health by way of a daily fitness regimen, but no matter how fit you get, you cannot stop there. Fitness is a fleeting thing, one without a clear final stage, and disappears when you stop working at it. Sure, if you are very healthy, you can take some time off without suffering any grave consequences, much like a company at the top of their game can allow themselves some indulgences, but these are only temporary pauses in an ongoing and never-ending struggle.

4. Talk is cheap, disruption is expensive. It will always be easier to call oneself a disruptor than actually doing any disrupting. This might sound like stating the obvious, but I present it as a way to start talking about the cost of disruption. While there is a tendency to play up the cheapness of entrepreneurship today, and the manner in which disruptors have managed to leverage inexpensive technologies to achieve great things, the reality is still that disruption comes at a price.

To begin with, disruptive innovation requires that you capitalize upon an emerging technology, and this will always have costs attached to it. These costs may be less than those of your competitors, but also includes costs related to learning the new way of working and developing a product or service in a distinctly different way.

This also points to how disruption comes with quite considerable cognitive costs. If you are an existing company, this might involve costs related to unlearning, costs related to entrenched technologies that need to be discounted, and organizational costs. If you are a new entrant, you will still need to pay the learning costs, not to mention the institutional costs that come with being a new player in an existing field. And we've not even touched upon the costs of educating and re-educating customers old and new, marketing a novel approach and making the new innovation scale.

5. Disruption isn't the easy way out, nor is it the cheap and cheerful way to innovate. It might be cheaper than it's alternative, but only because the alternative might be bankruptcy.

You'll always be far more likely to be disrupted than being a disruptor. At heart, the theory of disruption was always a theory about failure. Yes, it celebrated the clever upstart companies that managed to outfox the old guard, but more than this it was a story about how the very smart, the very knowledgeable, and the very well-financed still managed to miss and fail. The concept became beloved because it presented a tale in which the underdog won, in which the little guy conquered the big company, and in which there was always one more shot to take. It was a very American tale, one of upheaval and redemption, but the subtext is something more akin to a Greek tragedy.

Jill Lepore might have been right about the more upbeat promises of Christensen, or about the way in which disruption was turned into an almost cult-like tale of endless progress, but in attacking these points she missed out on the more fundamental aspect of the theory of disruptive innovation. This is the part where disruption is an updated term for a process identified by both Karl Marx and Joseph Schumpeter (if with very different readings), namely the notion that any and all institutions in the market economy are subject to creative destruction – "All that is solid melts into air, all that is holy is profaned"… Thus the theory of disruption shouldn't be read as gospel, i.e. as a tale of promise and resurrection. Instead, it should be read as something more like a *momento mori*, a reminder of our mortality. In fact, we might even say that the early (very early) precursors to The Innovator's Dilemma were the *ars moriendi text*s, medieval Latin works on the practice of dying well, read in order to meditate on our inherent limitations and the fact that any earthly success is only a temporary state.

The real lessons of disruption, then, aren't easy tricks with which to achieve innovation success, but rather the opposite. Disruption teaches us to be skeptical, to doubt sure things, to stay open to the fact that if you don't know who the fool is, the fool is you. The theory of disruption isn't necessarily a happy one, nor is it always motivational. It is realistic, and that might be the most disruptive thing of all.

About the author

 Alf Rehn (alfrehn.com) is Professor of Innovation, Design and Management at the University of Southern Denmark, sits on numerous boards of directors, and is a bestselling author and a strategic advisor for everything from hot new startups to Fortune 500 companies.

'EVEN IF YOU'RE ON THE RIGHT TRACK, YOU'LL GET RUN OVER IF YOU JUST SIT THERE.'

WILL ROGERS

ANTONIO NIETO-RODRIGUEZ

Focus, the differentiator

Look around. Think back to your organizational experience. I have done the same. Over three decades working in organizations and carrying out research into organizations, I have come to the conclusion that very few companies succeed in implementing their strategy.

Of course, some succeed in executing their strategies. My research suggests that what differentiates these companies from the others is that they have a great leader and a high maturity level in the key elements of their organization.

And there is another ingredient common to companies which execute strategy successfully: their ability to focus.

The reality is that most companies and many employees are highly unfocused. As a result, top management has difficulty setting and communicating a ranked list of priorities; and most staff members end up deciding on their own where to put their efforts, which will probably be on easy and rrelevant tasks. This lack of focus creates a huge amount of wasted money and resources, the inability to execute the strategy, project failures, and unhappy and uncommitted employees. Successful individuals are highly focused, and the same applies to organizations. While every business is focused when it is starting out, only those that manage to stay focused will succeed and stay in business.

So, what are the characteristics of a focused organization? To explain, I use FOCUSED as an acronym standing for:

F – Fewer projects, rather than many. A focused organization that is able to effectively select and prioritize its projects and invest in just a few good initiatives clearly outperforms organizations that take on too many projects and products. Some of greatest business leaders, like Steve Jobs, rightly comment that saying "No" is one of the most difficult tasks of a leader. Nevertheless, the leaders of an organization that wants to become focused will need to learn to say "No" to many initiatives.

O – Organized staff. In a focused enterprise, the staff is organized in such a way that all personnel know what is expected of them and how their work contributes to achievement of the strategy. They do not waste time on activities that are not part of their core skill set; rather, they focus on their key strengths and exploit the core competencies of the company.

C – Competitive mindset. The focused company competes with the outside world rather than internally. Internal competition is minimized because all of the organization's effort is placed on doing what it does best.

U – Urgency. In business, time flies—even more so with the current level of globalization. Organizations need to launch their initiatives quickly. The time-to-market for new products must become shorter and shorter. Creating a sense of "urgency" is a competitive advantage, and the focused organization is always aware of this fact.

S – Strategic alignment. Every initiative at a focused organization is linked to a strategic objective. Any project that is not so linked is immediately cancelled (my book *The Focused Organization* explains how to identify these projects and how to stop them).

E – Excellence. A focused organization applies the highest standards, and the key initiatives are managed by the best people. Employees understand the importance of quality and continuous improvement. With this approach, there is little room for internal politics.

D – Discipline. Companies today need discipline to execute their key initiatives; without it, consistent performance becomes very difficult. Of course, there is a need for creativity and flexibility as well. The challenge for the CEO and the company's entire management team is to find the right balance between discipline and creativity/flexibility.

An organization has to go through a large transformation project to become truly focused. It isn't easy. It demands time and resources, but the pay-offs are considerable. The most important benefits are these:

1. Achievement of strategic goals. Everybody in the focused organization, from the CEO to the accounts payable employee, knows the direction in which the organization is going, which two to three initiatives are the most important, and the business case for these few critical initiatives. All employees are extremely committed to helping the organization to become the best.

2. Increased agility and responsiveness to market changes. Identifying an optimal balance between the run-the-business and the change-the-business dimensions will bring lots of benefits to the organization. The result is that one plus one will be three. The organization will become agile and more responsive to market changes and competition. Eventually, the organization can become a trendsetter and market leader.

3. Happier and more engaged employees. Focus brings happiness to staff members: They know how to contribute to the company's success;, they are proud to belong to it; and they are ready to work harder. The fact that the company will be focused will create less tension and more harmony, and work will change from stressful and pressured to positive and rewarding. A healthy spirit will develop throughout the organization.

4. Positive financial results. This is probably the most important benefit of becoming a focused organization, since organizations need to have good financial results to survive and to please their shareholders. The focused organization reduces costs by cancelling those projects that are not relevant, a step that can result in huge savings. In addition, the focused organization chooses only those initiatives that will bring significant added value to the group

5. Higher performing organization. Project teams are clearly identified with the project objectives/goals and are willing to work hard because they enjoy what they are doing.

6. A culture of getting things done. Today, many organizations love to discuss new business initiatives, but they stop at the discussion stage. A focused organization selects just a few initiatives and gets them done.

Like all of the great business concepts, the case for focus is simple, irresistible and highly demanding to pull off. But that does not mean it can't be done. Indeed, to succeed in the long term, it must be done by any organization – or individual.

About the author

 Antonio Nieto-Rodriguez (antonionietorodriguez.com) is Director of the Programme Management Office at GlaxoSmithKline Vaccines and former chair of the Project Management Institute.

He is author of *The Focused Organization*; and has been teaching project management for more than a decade to senior executives at IE Business School, Duke CE, Solvay Business School and Vlerick. He was shortlisted for the 2017 Thinkers50 Ideas into Practice Award.

'STRATEGIES ARE INTELLECTUALLY SIMPLE; THEIR EXECUTION IS NOT.'

LARRY BOSSIDY

IN CONVERSATION

Rebecca Parsons

W hen it comes to getting things done, the business world has always been willing to embrace ideas and inspirations from a variety of sources. Military role models have proved perennially popular – from von Clausewitz on strategy to inspirations from US Navy SEALs. There is also a tradition of large organizations seeking out best practice from smaller businesses, and the entrepreneurial and creative worlds. Design Thinking, as exemplified by Ideo and others, has been studied over recent years. Similarly, the lean movement is now embraced by large corporations keen to import the combination of thrift, energy and creativity it extols.

Organizations are now looking for inspiration to those who are in the engine room of the digital revolution: the software developers and others who originate the technology which forms an increasingly important part of all of our lives.

Leading the way in this endeavour is the Agile Alliance. It has a simple and compelling manifesto:

"We are uncovering better ways of developing software by doing it and helping others do it. Through this work we have come to value individuals and interactions over processes and tools; working software over comprehensive documentation; customer collaboration over contract negotiation; and responding to change over following a plan."

As it has championed the working methods of developers, the Agile Alliance and the movement around it has spawned a new vocabulary – from Acceptance Test Driven Development (team members with different perspectives collaborating to write acceptance tests) to scrum (a process framework used to manage product development and other knowledge work) by way of pair programming (two programmers sharing a single workstation).

Among the most compelling and longest serving champions of agile thinking and practice is Rebecca Parsons, chief technology officer of ThoughtWorks. She has decades-long applications development experience across a range of industries and systems. Her technical track record includes leading the creation of large scale distributed object applications and the integration of disparate systems. She was previously a professor of computer science at the University of

Central Florida and also worked at the Los Alamos National Laboratory. She talked with Thinkers50 cofounder Stuart Crainer.

The Agile Alliance champions the way software is developed and holds it up as an example of how organizations can and perhaps should be organized. Is that a fair interpretation?

Yes, that's the next evolution. If you look at the whole evolution of how software was developed we started by dealing with problems which were relatively well understood – a payroll system, general ledger, and so on. Accounting systems haven't changed a great deal. Importantly the only people who worked with those systems were internal to companies. There weren't the same questions about usability. People learnt what they had to learn. You didn't have complex user interfaces and you could afford to decide upfront what exactly you were going to do because the rules and the models weren't changing. As those systems grew in size and complexity, we just kept building them in the same way. Everything we needed to do was settled in advance, then we designed something to do it, then built it and deployed it.

But those cycles were taking years and what started to happen, particularly as you got into the mid to late 1990s, was that things began changing rapidly. We started getting personal computers, client servers and more interactive interfaces, as well as more complex problems.

So, it became harder and harder to cast things in concrete. People began seeking out alternatives, even for large systems, and that is when the Agile Manifesto came along. And the basic premise was rather than seeing change as the enemy, we needed to look at change as inevitable and design processes that can respond more quickly to change. To do so, you need to get people collaborating more, you need rapid feedback.

Particularly as systems become more complex, it is actually more difficult for people to tell you exactly what they want. There were many instances where people would say, 'That is exactly what I asked for but it's not what I want'. Very often until you see something you can't know that it is not exactly what you wanted.

Feedback, collaboration and transparency are the basic underlying principles of the Agile Manifesto. It started out initially with software developers and then business analysts and testers. Increasingly, there was tight collaboration between the primary roles of software development and then we began spreading further out – you can see that recently in the DevOps movement.

Increasingly, it is about looking at bringing some of these agile principles and related practices to the operation of systems more broadly. How do you bring designers into this? How do you want to manage your entire portfolio of projects? And this is where you start to bump into strategy.

More and more companies are becoming technology companies that just happen to do business in insurance, manufacturing or retail banking. Almost every strategic change initiative will involve a change in an organization's technology.

So the question becomes how to apply those fine grain agile principles, honed over a couple of decades, around how to do software development, to the entire portfolio of an organization. It is about mapping between the strategic vision and what that implies to the business processes and the relationship between the organization, its customers and their partners. How do you translate that back into the changes you need to make in your technology and how can you most effectively implement that programme?

Transparency, feedback, openness, and the need for communication is something we've heard on many occasions, but it doesn't seem to penetrate the corporate core.

Yes, to some extent that is the legacy of organizational structures that were put in place in a different time.

And it is worth noting that there are challenges in an organization with complete transparency. You might have an executive committee weighing up different options about the future of the organization which might involve the closure of a plant or outsourcing work to another organization. If you are completely transparent during such deliberations you run the risk of demoralizing the different groups involved. You potentially pit them against each other.

You can look at the history of organizational dynamics and understand why you end up with cultures built around only disclosing the minimum necessary information. But that has become unfeasible in many ways because of how rapidly information moves around. With so much information publicly available it becomes increasingly difficult to be non-transparent. A lot of what organizations are struggling with now is how they operate when the default assumption is that some of these things will get out. It used to be security through obfuscation and ignorance. That doesn't work any more. Even if ignorance is widespread only one person has to figure it out and then everyone knows. If you are trying to hide something on the Internet behind some URL eventually someone will find it and as soon as they find it they will publicise it.

Organizations are having to go through this movement from how they used to be able to operate to how they need to operate now.

The historical and conventional view is that the agile concepts are all very well but difficult to scale: does that still hold true?

I think we're still experimenting about what it takes to scale agile to 50,000 or 100,000 developers. There are some frameworks out there but I don't consider it settled. There is still a lot about agile at the small scale which is still evolving.

One of the things about the Agile Alliance is that part of our mission is that we are not specific to any particular methodology. We refer to it as the big tent. Different organizations and certifying bodies look at a narrow slice. The role of the Agile Alliance is to be the big tent to allow practitioners of all of the different approaches to utilize agile across all the different roles and disciplines; to interact, to learn and teach each other, and to continue to evolve the use of these practices.

Are there cultural barriers within organizations to the understanding and practice of the Agile Manifesto?

When you start with the principles – feedback, transparency, collaboration – it is hard to argue against them. In practice sometimes it is culturally difficult. For example, pair programming might be difficult for people used to working by themselves who then find themself talking to someone else all day. But if you look at it another way it is simply rapid code review feedback. Someone is writing code, someone is looking at the code, they're then talking about what it should do, and questioning whether they have considered all the cases. So once you ground practice in the principle of rapid feedback then that starts to get over some of the cultural barriers.

One of the harder concepts is the notion of the self empowered team. In very hierarchical organizations and societies if you say that this motley crew of developers, analysts, testers, designers and so on can get together and organize themselves – as opposed to the project manager being in charge of all of the decision making – that is a difficult shift culturally. It is effectively giving up control. And people who have power and control generally don't like to give it up.

So there are some things that are culturally sensitive but in general I think the practices travel well. What we have also found is that as agile software development has become more accepted, the parts of the organization touched by software development begin to adapt these practices. So you have marketing campaigns being run in a lean style. I have seen people plan their wedding with a kanban board [a visual workflow tool consisting of multiple columns. Each column represents a different stage in the workflow process]! I know families that basically use the same sort of board to manage the chores that their children do.

These agile practices are in fact going out far from software development to many different kinds of activities

If you think about them from the context of the principles, it isn't that difficult to move those processes into completely unrelated fields. Our legal department at ThoughtWorks uses some of the agile software development practices in how they think about contracts. Of course, across industries, countries and roles the practices do change. It doesn't make sense to do pair programming to plan a wedding

Agile thinking appears to be in a sweet spot. There is overlap with the lean movement, the maker movement and design thinking for example.

Yes, it is certainly getting there and is definitely not the evil A-word it once was. I started working for ThoughtWorks in 1999 and many clients wanted to bring in this style of working but insisted we didn't use the word agile. You don't have to worry about that any more, but there are still questions. My response is that you might not do all of the practices but the principles are fundamental. You need to ground yourself in the principles.

For example, if you are creating software to make medical diagnoses if you get it wrong people might die. So, you need to bring a different level of rigour than you would do if you were creating software for a sandwich ordering system. But you still need to have feedback, you still need to regularly and rigorously test what you are doing, and need extensive collaboration between people who are working on different parts of the system so that they truly understand the underlying assumptions. You might do the practices differently but that does not mean you are not following the principles and values.

That is definitely becoming more accepted and is allowing the Agile Alliance and the concepts to branch out to different parts of organizations. This is also influencing the way strategy is thought about. A strategic plan that doesn't show any concrete change for five years is highly incompatible with an agile and lean way of thinking.

Now people are thinking about applying the concept of a Minimum Viable

Product to strategy. [A Minimum Viable Product is, as Eric Ries said, the "version of a new product which allows a team to collect the maximum amount of validated learning about customers with the least effort."] How can we break strategy into different streams? How can we build feedback cycles into strategy so we know early on that the strategic change is achieving the strategic changes we want? Lean thinking, flow thinking and the concepts of feedback from agile are all part of how you take a strategic vision and turn it into a strategic change programme. And that is how this realm of agile thinking is moving into the strategy arena.

Over the last century companies have mastered how to create strategy, but it seems that in the software development world you have mastered the art of implementation. Now it seems the two are meeting each other.

The whole process of agile software development is to take a higher-level articulation of what your business level requirements are and translate them into implementable chunks of technology. This is taking it further: how do you decompose a strategic change initiative into different streams and business requirements to get feedback?

There are all sorts of implementation aspects of any strategic change initiative – technology, process change, the introduction of new partners into an ecosystem and so on. But by using the mindset of decomposing -- in order to get transparency and feedback on how the processes are working and how successfully they are being executed – this entire collection of ideas can influence the implementation of strategic vision

It seems that software development's role in the modern society is actually overlooked.

Yes, I think so. Increasingly it is what keeps the technological age going. More and more industries are being defined by technology. Differentiation between companies in the same industry is being driven by their ability to adapt new technology and to adapt to new technology. And that is going to continue.

Think about airlines and their ability to recover after a bad storm. It is a logistics problem but also a technology problem. More and more industries are having to think about their business in the context of their technology, their grasp of technology and technology's ability to help them differentiate themselves from their competitors.

What still excites you?

One of the things I like is that it is still extremely dynamic. As we are addressing new problems we have to think about how we are going to approach those problems. It is still constantly changing and that is what I always loved about technology.

'THE REAL CHALLENGE
IN CRAFTING STRATEGY
LIES IN DETECTING THE
SUBTLE DISCONTINUITIES
THAT MAY UNDERMINE
A BUSINESS IN THE
FUTURE. AND FOR THAT
THERE IS NO TECHNIQUE,
NO PROGRAMME, JUST
A SHARP MIND IN TOUCH
WITH THE SITUATION.'

HENRY MINTZBERG

DOMINIC HOULDER & NANDU NANDKISHORE

Five questions to ask of your purpose

Corporate purpose needs asserting and defending as never before. In a world of scepticism, clarity of purpose and consistency in living that purpose will powerfully differentiate a company from its competitors – in the market for customers and talent. More fundamentally, as organizations face stronger cross winds, with high levels of volatility in every area of corporate activity, the what and how will need to change frequently. This leaves purpose – the answer to the question why – as the primary compass for navigating key decisions.

Companies need to constantly ask themelves five key questions:

1: Is your purpose worth defending?

Not if it's just a set of words. Statements of purpose often float upwards into fluffy, generic moral injunctions, or land heavily as marketing slogans and value propositions. The sweet spot is where a definition of purpose brings value and values together. It must be a business purpose – that is, built around what the organization can deliver – but its roots must be in morality, in the sense of being outward looking and being of service to others: consumers, society, and employees, not just shareholders.

Purpose is often buried in an organization's history and the memories of its founders. Nestlé was founded to save the life of a baby. Soichiro Honda and his business partner Takeo Fujisawa founded their company to restore Japanese pride in engineering, rather than military achievement. Sam Walton looked to bring value to out-of-the-way places.

The stories that employees tell each other about their history – especially foundation stories – are potent carriers of the purpose that is worth defending: much more so than the products of corporate identity consultants.

A worthwhile purpose leads to action. Ove Arup, founder of the global engineering and architecture practice, wrote "The Key Speech", which to this day is mandatory reading for all new employees. The speech sets out Arup's purpose to advance excellence in engineering – and to turn down any project, however lucrative, which fails to advance that aim. Arup's purpose is both bold and practical, organizational and personal. For example, it warns employees to expect only second quartile remuneration, but unparalleled access to knowledge for their own development. Arup's governance lends steel to its purpose: Ove Arup gave all his equity to the Arup Foundation, which owns the firm and whose objective is the advancement of excellence.

Undoubtedly, a purpose worth defending brings dilemmas. A company for example, could set its core purpose as delivering fresh and nutritious food to enhance people's health. Would the acquisition of a fast food burger business go beyond those boundaries? If the purpose is meaningful, consumers – and ultimately employees – will respond with anger or disengagement if top executives subvert it.

2: Are you communicating your purpose?

It's not the words that count; it's what they do. Far too much time, energy and money is devoted to word-smithing slogans. Slogans won't carry a purpose, but stories will. The CEO needs to be the Chief Storytelling Officer, inspiring managers who retell the stories of foundation, hard choices, dilemmas, conflicts and victories that build the organization's mythology.

This often requires skills which may be new to many corporate chiefs, but it is essential to develop them. The story need not be slick, and the telling doesn't have to be charismatic. The point is that it is authentic, in the sense of belonging to the organization and those who have lived within it, rather than being just the property of the top team or, worse, their advisers.

Communication needs a good listener as well as a good story teller: can your organization listen? It's hard to listen to a story told at the wrong organizational level. At Blue Circle Industries, a global construction materials business that is now part of Lafarge Holcim, top management struggled to communicate a purpose that could resonate across all parts of its highly diversified portfolio. The search for common ground led to a very generic statement of purpose. This focused on delivering shareholder value and was wrapped in the familiar moral grandstanding of prizing integrity, creativity and so on. The statement of purpose was relevant only at the level of the holding company. It failed to register in the ears of those delivering customer value across the range of different contexts in the company.

And the timing needs to be right. The organization needs to be ready to hear about purpose. When Harvey Golub was turning round American Express in the 1990s, he famously said that if he had tried to communicate a sense of purpose he would have seemed to have arrived from the planet Mars. Ultimately the company's purpose was to become the world's most respected service brand, but when AmEx was in deep trouble with a brand sinking rapidly what was needed was not so much a statement of purpose as a set of clear, concrete, credible priorities for action. In this case, introspection around purpose would have lacked any credibility, and execution around the basics of cost management and integration had to be at the top of the agenda, for at least Golub's first two years.

3: What's fixed and what's up for grabs?

The definition of the business you are in can change over time, sometimes dramatically. Diageo, the global drinks company, had its roots in the Grand Met-Guinness merger. Grand Met – at the time of the merger already a prominent drinks business – had very different origins. Its founder, Maxwell Joseph, began in the hotels business in the 1940s, progressing through property trading into dairies, restaurants, pubs and so into liquor. Curiously, at the same time, the Bass Group evolved in the opposite direction: from brewing into hotels.

Within a business, the strategy can and will change – at an increasing velocity as we move further into a complex and uncertain future.

What does that mean for purpose? Purpose is not the same as business definition nor the same as strategy – but both of these are an expression of what the business stands for. So, as your company navigates changes in strategy and portfolio composition do not fail to re-examine your purpose: to what extent are you reaching its limits? A big mistake is to assume that purpose is fixed for all time: only a generic purpose can be unchanging.

When business environments change dramatically, or when organizations lose their way, studying and understanding the past can be very instructive. The twists and turns of strategy and business definition over the years prove excellent material for questioning and rediscovering what your purpose was in hindsight, and where you might have strayed from it. This, in turn, enables a corrective, future facing perspective on purpose.

Minding the past allows us to recall times of particularly strong (or weak) stakeholder engagement and what drove it. Considering key turning points in the organization's history can expose deeply embedded patterns of behaviour. The early history of Honda, for example, is replete with stories of failure and the unexpected. Honda's legendary US market entry in the late 1950s was not the result of a planned strategy but apparent accident. The preferred product category failed and small, lightweight motorbikes – that nobody at Honda intended to sell in the US, but which executives had kept for their personal use

– were spotted by a Sears buyer. Those stories point to and bring to life a purpose of transformation through learning, persistence and a non-punitive culture.

4: Have you planned for your purpose being subverted?

Subversion typically comes from short term pressures. Fundamental commitments may well be jettisoned to address a crisis or make up for shortfalls against immediate performance promises. The price is a loss of credibility across key stakeholder groups. As those pressures will inevitably come, it is important to plan for them.

One key is to create watchdogs, who will bark loudly when purpose is violated. The Hershey Foundation, for example, recruited John Scharffenberger to act as the company's guardian and ambassador to cocoa growers in West Africa. Scharffenberger had sold Hershey his eponymous boutique, ethical chocolate brand. As well as the product, Hershey sought to retain this distinctive voice as a forceful reminder to the company of what it stood for. Similarly, the accounting firm PwC retains the firm's wisest elders after retirement on the firm's supervisory boards, as custodians of purpose in the context of a partnerial culture.

Looking to past commitments can help to anchor your organization's purpose: so can looking to the future, as emerging trends will reinforce or challenge it. Reverse mentoring from outsiders is also useful. Credible youngsters can hold your statement of purpose up to the scrutiny of stakeholders. Ask them to imagine and tell the story of your organization's (hypothetical) "death", and co-create the story of its "rebirth".

5: Is the organization's purpose connected to your own?

Buddhist tradition speaks of the Buddha's teaching on rebirth. He compared this to a flame being passed from candle to candle. The flame is different, but also the same. So it is with purpose across the generations. As a leader, you are the channel for your organization's purpose and if it fails to connect with you it can hardly connect with others.

The corporate purpose answers the organization's "why?" question; but what about your own? What is the link between your personal story and the story told about your company? One key to ensuring connection is to focus on your legacy. The legacy of purpose bears your personal imprint as a leader. As you pass it on, it will change but retain its roots in what you contributed and in what earlier generations brought to you.

These measures for monitoring purpose have to be combined with strong governance processes to ensure that the company stays on track. In this context, an important point to be kept in mind is the gap which frequently appears between short and long-term strategy. Most companies are good at articulating a long-term vision and strategy, based on the company purpose, they are also good at developing robust processes to ensure that short term deliverables enable them to meet financial KPIs. Where companies tend to fall short is in the medium term strategy, to bridge the short term and the long term.

About the authors

Dominic Houlder is an Adjunct Professor of Strategic and International Management at London Business School.

Nandu Nandkishore is an Executive Fellow at London Business School. Previously he was an executive board director of Nestlé S.A.

This is an edited version of an article which first appeared in the online edition of the *Harvard Business Review*.

'STRATEGY IS EXTRAORDINARILY EMOTIONAL AND DEMANDING. IT IS NOT A RITUAL OR A ONCE-A-YEAR EXERCISE, THOUGH THAT IS WHAT IT HAS BECOME. WE HAVE SET THE BAR TOO LOW.'

GARY HAMEL

ESSENTIAL THINKER

Pankaj Ghemawat

Pankaj Ghemawat is based at New York's Stern School and IESE Business School in Spain. Prior to that he was the youngest full professor at Harvard Business School. His 2011 book *World 3.0* (Harvard Business Review Press, 2011) won the Thinkers50 Book Award.

Ghemawat is the Global Professor of Management and Strategy and director of the Center for the Globalization of Education and Management at the Stern School of Business, and the Anselmo Rubiralta Professor of Global Strategy at IESE Business School.

Ghemawat's books include *Commitment* (Harvard Business Review Press, 1991); *Games Businesses Play* (Harvard Business Review Press, 1997); *Strategy and the Business Landscape* (Harvard Business Review Press, 1999); and *Redefining Global Strategy* (Harvard Business Review Press, 2007).

His latest book, *The Laws of Globalization and Business Applications* (Cambridge University Press, 2016) provides a rigorous data-driven discussion of globalization at the world, country, industry and firm levels. Ghemawat's next book, *The New Global Road Map: Enduring Strategies for Turbulent Times* (forthcoming in 2018 from Harvard Business Review Press), will explain the key trends affecting global business today and how globalization levels around the world are changing.

Ghemawat is also the lead author of the DHL Global Connectedness Index, a comprehensive analysis of the state of globalization across 140 countries.

Pankaj Ghemawat

When you speak to people about globalization what is the thing that really mystifies them or that they don't understand?

Well, I think right now we're living in an environment of tremendous ambiguity about where globalization is headed. There is just more than the usual amount of disagreement about is it up, is it down, is it going sideways? That seems like an essential precursor for any company to try to decide how it should adjust its strategy in light of what's going on.

You research and publish the DHL Global Connectedness Index, which basically shows that the world is less globalized than we might like to think.

Yes, given the ambiguity about perceptions I prefer to focus on data or facts. The DHL Global Connectedness Index is based on roughly about two million data points. It looks both at the depth of globalization and the breadth of globalization, not just how much stuff crosses borders but how far it goes. It's the only globalization index out there that actually picked up the global financial crisis of 2008, which gives us a little bit more confidence that it is responsive to shifts in the environment.

Basically what the 2016 edition of the Global Connectedness Index indicated is that despite the huge downturn in media sentiment about globalization, globalization has basically gone sideways over the last few years. It's not broken bad, nor has it clearly broken a ceiling to head towards new levels, particularly when we focus on trade and FDI. So we're in a little bit of a suspenseful period of doldrums, as it were, when depending on what happens in the political sphere you could imagine things picking up, but you could also imagine things coming down a bit.

In the past there was a feeling that globalization had a kind of energy behind it, it was an unstoppable juggernaut, but now it seems that the media and the politicians are changing the agenda, in a surprising way, because it did seem unstoppable.

Well, it seemed unstoppable to some people. So, when I wrote my 2007 book, *Redefining Global Strategy*, the great and the good were generally convinced that the world was either flat or soon about to become flat. If you keep a little bit of historical perspective on this you see that periods of great excitement about globalization are usually followed by disappointment, and this is not the only such instance I can think. To just focus on the 25 years that I've been focused on globalization. Think of what happened when the Berlin Wall came down – huge excitement. Think of how it ended – with the Asian crisis. And what's interesting is some of the implications for companies that people were talking about back at the time of the Asian crisis and which turned out not to work very well are exactly the kinds of remedies that people are talking about in the current situation.

So, the world is not flat but unpleasantly bumpy?

Unpleasantly bumpy or grumpy or whatever you want to call it, but definitely assuming that borders don't matter and that distance doesn't matter are two very bad ideas.

Can you expand on that – why are they bad ideas?

Well, I think that first of all if you don't recognise the bumps, the joint effect of the border and distance effects, you basically end up with strategies that, to quote Dr Seuss, involve figuring on biggering the enterprise without paying any attention to how you might have to change your strategy, how you might want to decide where to compete versus where not to compete, and so forth. Or another way of putting is if you ignore borders and distances your basic strategy is bigger and blander, and that doesn't work too well – so that would be one reason.

I think the second reason why believing that borders and distances have stopped mattering is that at a public policy level it suggests to us that there's nothing to be gained from further integration and it's only if you recognise that there are still significant obstacles to crossing borders that you realise that there might be scope, for instance, for, say, trade facilitation arrangements that might further increase global welfare. So, both at the level of public policy and at the level of business strategy seem to be some compelling reasons why you want to be realistic about this rather than simply go with the flow and repeat whatever is being said about globalization.

Jeff Immelt at GE talks about the company's bold pivot from globalization to localization – is that a credible, useful response, do you think?

Well, I talk a little bit about Jeff's speech, the one that he gave at NYU at commencement in May 2016, because I was there, and I was surprised. Jeff is of course a more nuanced thinker than the bold pivot to localization would suggest so now he's started talking about connected localization.

But the point is that, first of all, in general terms these were exactly the kinds of responses we heard last time before the global financial crisis, that things got bad during the Asian currency crisis. Coke, in particular, decided that it was over-standardized and so Douglas Daft, who had just taken over as CEO, put in a think local, act local strategy. It was a disaster in terms of what it did to Coke's headquarter capabilities, in terms of the leeway it allowed underprepared country managers to prepare really questionable ads, a whole range of problems, and it's only when Neville Isdell took over a couple of years later that he kind of righted the balance, neither the extreme standardization under Goizueta nor the extreme localization that Daft was talking about.

And so when I look at suggestions that localization is the answer I think, first of all, as to how well this worked the last time around. And second, the other thing I think of is that frankly, especially for a company like GE, which has chosen to be in scale sensitive businesses, how do you really localize jet engines? – not entirely clear to me.

One thing that becomes clear in your research is there are very few successful global companies who are successful in different regions. You site Honda as one of the few examples – it's successful in Asia, North America and Europe, but it's amazing that there are so few that you consider to be globally successful, even though we would consider them to be global organizations.

Yes, it is quite striking because the general pattern that you see when you look across many multinationals is they make money at home and lose it overseas, and it's a little bit of a reminder that globalization is not an imperative, it's something that you need to subject to cost-benefit analysis and something that you need to think about carefully in terms of where you're going to compete, how you're going to do so, and so forth.

So, this morning, I was speaking to a law firm and since that example is much on my mind, let's just think of legal services where many people have talked about globalization. There have been a whole bunch of trans-Atlantic mergers, etc. The basic regularity that you see when you look at the data from American Lawyer, etc, is that at least for the US firms profit per equity partner is significantly negatively related to the percentage of equity partners outside the US. So clearly for most law firms the assumption that globalization was automatically going to be a profitable strategy hasn't worked out.

In contrast, this morning I was with a company called Clyde & Co, which actually is quite successful as a multi-country law firm. They've been named the trans-Atlantic law firm of the year two years running, and their whole thing was they found a niche, shipping and insurance, and worked around that. That niche has proven to be quite globalizable and Clyde & Co does well, despite having most of its equity partners outside its home base in the UK.

And so I think that another problem with global-only of the sort associated with saying borders don't matter, distance doesn't matter, is it's just an invitation to go out there without having done the necessary homework and without having asked yourself the hard questions of whether globalization makes sense for you given where you're coming from and where you're trying to compete and how.

These are fundamental business questions and so it's a bit astonishing that CEOs aren't asking themselves the questions.

Well, I think the CEO sometimes is stuck in a dual role that makes it complicated. A number of the CEOs I know see it as their personal responsibility to help make the organization more global, partly because they sense resistance a bit lower down within the organization, maybe not their direct reports, maybe two levels down.

So it's a little bit hard to be the analyst and the motivator at the same time. So, in fact, when we do global-only surveys, the last one I did where we broke things out between CEOs and non-CEOs, CEOs were inclined to overstate actual levels of globalization by an even greater amount than the other people in our sample, not because presumably they have less experience but presumably because they're a bit torn between being analytical and trying to persuade other people within their organization to actually get a move on.

Who's doing this well do you think? You must come across organizations where you think, yes, they've really thought about it and are doing intelligent things.

Yes. Well, I think, again, it's way easier to make lists of companies that aren't doing this well than companies that are doing it well. But if I think to some of the companies that I find most interesting right now I think that in IT services you see some great examples, both from the West and from emerging economies — companies that know better than to get distracted by all this noise about the end of arbitrage, that's the core of the Indian business model. These are companies that are pretty clear that they know what they're going to do no matter what kinds of restrictions get put on to H-1B visas in the United States.

Similarly, IBM and Accenture are not going to stress arbitrage because arbitrage is a loaded word, but the reason that they have a hundred thousand-plus employees each in India means that they understand what the critical things are in their business and the need, even though they are differentiated players, to at least be in the cost ballpark vis-à-vis their Indian competitors.

I find companies like Cemex, which admittedly did do a very, very ill-starred acquisition of Rinker just before the financial crisis, reminding us that nobody is immune from doing dumb things. But when I think of the other things they have been doing, how selective they've become again about their portfolios, about the kind of emphasis that the late Lorenzo Zambrano put on really multinationalizing the top management team, etc, they've gone very, very far compared to many companies from advanced economies in terms of how cosmopolitan and how able to manage across differences they've become.

So, there are some of the traditional powerhouses that continue to do well, typically in businesses where scale matters a great deal and affords them protection from local competitors. There are also some scrappy new challengers, whether it's the Indian IT firms, Cemex, or even Lenovo, which I think has done a very good job with a very different capital cost than IBM of taking that ThinkPad business and really figuring out how to maintain it as a global brand.

One thought that I'll add, one of the indicators that I look for as perhaps the single most powerful indicator ahead of time as to how well a company is going to be able to actually work across borders is I look at the level of cosmopolitism of the top management team, and it turns out that the for the Fortune Global 500, because we painstakingly went and did this analysis for every Fortune Global 500 company we could get our hands on, they are less globalized along that dimension than on any other dimension that we measured them on.

So, I think that it's a pretty good sign that if the CEO is a non-native, well, that means roughly about half the top management team will be non-native as well. That kind of company strikes me as probably better suited to deal with the challenges that globalization might throw up than a company where the CEO is native, where on average ninety per cent of the top management team, the direct reports, are natives as well. So, there are almost these two clusters of companies, the kind of run by natives, and the ones that actually do have some significant injection of talent from outside, and I think that this is actually one of the areas where we're going to have to pay more attention if we want to improve companies' globalization experiences.

Are you optimistic?

Over the long run I'm optimistic because when I think of how long the process of economic integration has been underway and how big the potential gains still are, without quite being teleologically minded, I can see a lot of momentum behind this process. In the short to medium run I'm in way more cautious mode, and so it's a little bit like I can predict that in the long run the climate is probably going to be conducive to firms that follow global strategies that are well thought out – in the short run the weather is a little bit hard to predict.

'STRATEGIC PLANNING, AT BEST, IS ABOUT POSING QUESTIONS, MORE THAN ATTEMPTING TO ANSWER THEM.'

RICHARD PASCALE

LOIZOS HERACLEOUS

Agility for the strategist: the SLO framework

Agility is the fashion of the day. Companies in industries as diverse as information technology, finance, hospitality and manufacturing operate agility programmes. The challenge is, however, that nobody seems to have a clear idea of what agility is or what it entails; and those who do, tend to disagree with others in the know. This is hardly surprising given the multiple roots of agility. Becoming popular as a way to organise software coding efforts in a flexible, client-oriented and scalable way, agility was initially inspired by the Toyota Production System, the "rugby" approach to innovation, and even prior total quality management principles taught by Deming.

The "Agile Manifesto", created in 2001 by 17 software engineers in Utah, codified some principles of software development such as "ndividuals and interactions over processes and tools", "responding to change over following a plan" and "working software over comprehensive documentation". These principles make sense, but they appear more operational and relevant to software development than assuaging the concerns of the strategist wondering how agile their organization is or what agile actually means from a strategic point of view.

In my work with organizations including NASA's Johnson Space Center, I have developed a framework that can help to pin down agility for strategists and leaders. In 2014 the Johnson Space Center initiated a programme referred to as JSC 2.0 that aims to make the Center "more lean, agile and adaptive to change". I created the SLO framework as a way to spur strategic conversations about what agility might mean and entail.

From the strategist's point of view, agility is about one of the central challenges of organizations: adapting to changing circumstances. Leaders should be able to sense signals, evaluate them and take initiative; re-configure the organization accordingly and in alignment with the strategy, also subject to amendment as needed. Each of the three elements of strategy, leadership and organization (hence the SLO framework) is necessary but not sufficient; only synergy among the three can enable a company to be truly agile.

Agile leaders are those who can raise their perspective from the day-to-day, sense signals, reflect on the implications of those signals, and then spur initiatives to drive their organization to do what's needed. A variety of organizational features such as routines, worldviews and sunk costs continuously operate against this process.

In this sense agile leaders are champions of questioning accepted truths. Elon Musk may be the archetype of such a leader. His initiatives in space exploration, electronic vehicles, solar energy and even tunnel-building in cities reveal his ability to read signals of what is needed and what is possible, work out the implications and then lead initiatives to take things forward, doing so in novel ways and surmounting obstacles that would stop others in their tracks.

From a strategic perspective, agile organizations are able to overcome inertia and reshape their business models, balance change and stability, and build inter-organizational networks to push forward learning and influence their environments. Re-shaping business models is most often a long-term task that entails ongoing commitment. IBM's long-term shifts from a hardware producer to a solutions provider and currently to a "cognitive solutions and cloud platform provider" is one example. GE's various strategic shifts over the decades, such as portfolio re-shaping, the move from a manufacturing focus to service businesses, and currently its focus on becoming a digital enterprise, is another. At a strategic level agility does not have to be immediate, and indeed it cannot be for large corporations. It takes time to change the direction of a steamer. Corporations require both periodic strategic changes over time, while at the same time re-configuring their operations to maintain efficiency and responsiveness; one manifestation of the elusive capability of ambidexterity.

Finally, organizational agility requires experimentation, cross-functional collaboration, re-allocation of resources to support exploration, learning, as well as active un-learning of routines and processes that are no longer relevant. Alphabet may be the archetype of an agile organization. A multitude of experiments take place; some fail (Google Glass, Dodgeball), some go on to create new multi-billion dollar markets (Google Search, Google Play), and some are emerging, showing immense promise (DeepMind, that will support a multitude of offerings supported by AI). Alphabet learns and also unlearns, shutting down experiments that don't show results and reallocates resources to those that do. At any time, many flowers are allowed to bloom, and some of those will fill the valley.

The framework, right, can allow strategists to evaluate their company's agility levels and pinpoint where attention should be focused. The elements of the framework can spur strategic conversations about agility by asking the right

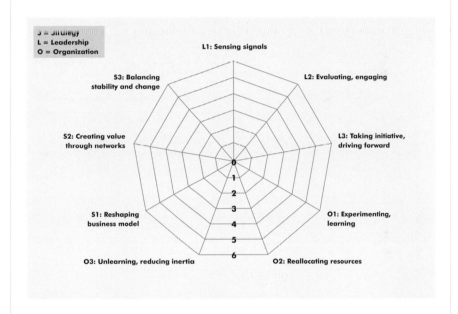

© Loizos Heracleous

questions about essential capabilities. These nine elements fit together like a jigsaw puzzle. Take one out, and the likelihood of achieving agility is diminished. The synergy across these components is what can lead to results. This framework boils down several agility-related concepts to their essence, in a way that can help strategists and leaders pin down what it means, evaluate their organization, and take action.

About the author

 Loizos Heracleous is a professor of strategy at Warwick Business School and an associate fellow at Green Templeton College, University of Oxford. He earned his PhD from the University of Cambridge. He is the author of several books and co-editor of *Agility.X* (Cambridge University Press, 2018). More information about Loizos can be found at www.heracleous.org and @Strategizing.

'IT'S A MYTH THAT INNOVATION IS EXTREMELY RISKY AND COSTLY – IN FACT, INNOVATION IS ONLY AN EXPENSIVE GAMBLE WHEN YOU DO IT WRONG. TODAY THE KNOWLEDGE, TOOLS AND PROCESSES EXIST TO SYSTEMATICALLY REDUCE THE MARKET RISK INHERENT TO NEW IDEAS, BUSINESS MODELS, AND VALUE PROPOSITIONS.'

ALEX OSTERWALDER & YVES PIGNEUR

ANDRÁS TILCSIK

Management in the age of meltdowns

On April 20, 2010, mud began gushing out of the well onto the drilling floor at Deepwater Horizon. Seconds later a geyser of water and mud sprayed up inside the derrick at the center of the giant rig; gas sensors went off everywhere; and the lights went out. One explosion was followed by a second, bigger blast, and a fireball, hundreds of feet high, enveloped the rig. Eleven workers died in the accident that night, and the blowout that caused the explosions sent 200 million gallons of oil gushing into the Gulf of Mexico in one of the worst environmental disasters in history. BP's costs associated with the spill: more than $50 billion.

Other catastrophes aren't physical but digital. When the markets opened on August 1, 2012, the Knight Capital Group was one of Wall Street's largest traders, but less than an hour later the company was on the brink of collapse. A software glitch had caused the firm's trading system to go haywire and flood the market with four million unintended orders, resulting in Knight Capital acquiring several billion dollars in unwanted positions. When the firm eventually sold back those stocks, it had lost $460 million — roughly $200,000 per each second of the trading meltdown. By the next day, three-quarters of Knight Capital's market value had been erased. The firm scrambled to avoid collapse and was eventually acquired by a competitor.

Disasters like BP's oil spill and Knight Capital's trading meltdown can threaten the very existence of even the largest of corporations. And such failures aren't limited to high-stakes, exotic domains like deep-water drilling and electronic trading. From food-safety accidents in restaurant chains to defect recalls affecting car manufacturers, failures abound in ordinary industries and can devastate profits, trigger legal actions, and cause lasting reputational damage.

To make matters worse, these dangers are increasing, according to many business leaders. In a recent survey of more than 1,000 executives in a wide range of industries, nearly 60 per cent reported that the volume and complexity of the risks their organizations face have increased substantially in the past half-decade. At the same time, only a minority reported that their organization had implemented a complete firm-wide process for enterprise risk management.

So, what can executives do to reduce the risk of catastrophic failures in their organizations? Traditional risk management steps — such as instituting rules and controls, scenario planning, and bringing in additional experts — can be quite helpful, but they have their limitations as the complexity increases. For example, a rule-based approach — identifying the things that could go wrong, instituting procedures to prevent them, and enforcing those procedures through monitoring — often fails to capture the breadth of potential risks and may instead foster a punitive culture that causes people to conceal risks. The use of scenario planning to identify risks is a more sophisticated approach, but it has problems of its own, sometimes leading decision makers to focus on a potentially narrow set of risks and responses based on scenarios that are vivid and easy to imagine. All too often, scenario planning also fails to capture the messy complexity of interconnected systems and organizations, as well as the chaos and fallibility of crisis responses. Research in numerous industries likewise reveals fundamental limits of relying on expert ability. For example, teams dominated by subject-matter experts are often vulnerable to group overconfidence and might suppress valuable input from non-expert skeptics. Such group dynamics are especially likely to yield bad outcomes in complex and uncertain environments.

At the same time, researchers are increasingly uncovering other interventions that can improve decisions, strengthen complex systems, and reduce catastrophic risks. In our book, *Meltdown: Why Our Systems Fail and What We Can Do About It*, Chris Clearfield and I discuss several best practices in depth; here's a summary of a few of them:

1. **Learn from incidents.** In complex systems, it's impossible to predict all of the possible paths to catastrophe. But even so, there are often emerging signals that can bring to light any interactions and risks that might otherwise be unexpected and hidden. Indeed, a timeline of the weeks and months leading up to a major failure is often a history of smaller failures, near misses, glaring irregularities, and other indications that something might be amiss. Incident tracking is a powerful way to learn from such signals, and there are notable success cases. In healthcare and aviation, for example, effective incident reporting systems help managers sort through the overwhelming haystack of possible warning signs to identify sources of potentially catastrophic errors. In recent years, such systems have proliferated in other industries as well. But these systems are effective only if employees feel safe enough to report issues and if the output is actually used to generate insights

and effect change. To do so, it's essential to designate a specific group, with sufficient understanding of operational concerns, to sort through, analyze, and prioritize incoming information. In the absence of this, insights can be lost even when critical data are available. Moreover, once information is recorded and analyzed, people must use it to generate insights about the root causes of those incidents and to fix problems without delay, rather than simply relegating it to a risk report. Emerging insights can then be disseminated throughout the organization. When used in this way, incident reporting systems can enable decision makers to anomalize, that is, to treat minor errors and lapses as distinctive and potentially significant details rather than as normal, familiar events.

2. **Encourage dissent.** Insiders often have serious reservations about the decisions or procedures in place well before a major accident, but they either fail to share these concerns or are ignored by managers. Many of those who observe these indications – typically, employees on the front lines – feel uncomfortable disclosing errors, expressing dissenting views, and questioning established procedures. To counter these tendencies, it's important for leaders to cultivate what researcher Amy Edmondson calls psychological safety: a shared belief among team members that the group will not admonish or penalize individuals for speaking up and challenging established procedures or widely held views. Psychological safety requires a climate in which team members trust and respect one another regardless of differences in their formal status. Research has shown that, through their words and actions, executives can do a great deal to foster psychological safety in a team or even within an entire organization. This requires that leaders credibly signal that they are willing to consider and address challenging questions and dissenting voices openly and productively, rather than defensively. These kinds of leadership behaviours help demonstrate that it's safe to raise questions, to admit mistakes, and to disagree with the team's consensus – critical steps in understanding where hidden dangers might be lurking in a complex system.

3. **Use structured decision tools.** One way to reduce the number of small errors that might cascade into larger failures is to mitigate the effect of cognitive biases in decision making. The use of structured decision tools, rather than intuitive thinking, can lessen the influence of some of those biases. Cognitive psychologists, for example, have proposed a list of questions that

executives can use to detect and minimize the effect of cognitive biases when making major decisions based on a recommendation from their team. For example, is the worst case bad enough? Were dissenting opinions adequately explored? And could the diagnosis of the situation have been overly influenced by salient analogies? Many of these questions are quite straightforward and seemingly obvious but, in practice, they are rarely raised explicitly. A checklist ensures that these questions are actually considered, thus helping executives to apply quality control to their decisions. Similarly, decision tools can also reduce the effect of cognitive biases in predictions. For instance, a simple tool called Subjective Probability Interval EStimates (SPIES) has been shown to produce less overconfident estimates than do unstructured, intuitive forecasting approaches.

4. **Diversify teams.** Teams composed of individuals with diverse professional backgrounds and expertise can be an effective risk management strategy. Research on bank boards, for example, suggests that banks with some non-expert directors – those with a background in other fields such as in law, the public sector, or the military – tend to be less likely to fail than banks with directors who all come from a banking background. It seems that having a mix of industry experts and non-experts can serve as effective safeguard against overconfidence on a board. These outsiders often raise inconvenient questions and force bankers on the board to justify their proposals and explain why formerly unacceptable risks might have become acceptable. In addition, even surface-level diversity – diversity in team members' visible characteristics like sex, age, and race – might help reduce the overconfidence of decision makers. Recent research, for example, suggests that the mere presence of ethnic diversity can reduce overconfidence in the actions of others, thus fostering greater scrutiny and more deliberate thinking.

5. **Conduct risk reviews.** A risk review is a structured audit of an organization by external investigators who gather qualitative and quantitative data to uncover hidden and unexpected risks to the organization. The investigators, who are typically independent experts on risk management in complex systems and organizations, begin the review by conducting confidential interviews with a variety of personnel at different levels in the organizational hierarchy, from higher-level executives to junior employees working on the front lines. The goal of these interviews is to reveal potential risks that might

not be visible at a given hierarchical level or within a particular organizational silo. The interviews can also provide an indication of the willingness of employees to share their concerns and dissenting opinions with supervisors. Next, to examine the most important issues raised in the confidential interview process, the investigators gather additional qualitative or quantitative data from surveys, additional interviews, or the organization's archives. Because a risk review leverages independent generalist experts and cuts across hierarchical and bureaucratic boundaries within the organization, it's particularly suitable for uncovering risks that are created by internal decision-making processes and organizational structures.

It's also an effective guard against risk creep. Although the gradual slide toward increasingly risky practices tends to be imperceptible to insiders, outsiders can often recognize it and help ensure that unacceptable risks are challenged and mitigated. Of course, a risk review will only be effective if executives are open to the investigators' conclusions, even if that information might occasionally be uncomfortable, disconcerting, and perhaps painful to hear. Otherwise the investigators' main advantage – their independent external perspective, allowing them to question industry and company assumptions and conventional practices, to poke holes in arguments, and to disagree with the existing consensus – can easily be lost.

6. **Develop more realistic contingency plans.** It's essential for organizations to develop robust crisis planning and response capabilities. During that process, executives need to recognize that estimates for worst-case scenarios are often explicitly or implicitly built from information that is biased by observations of recent orderly behaviour and the assumption that the mitigations outlined in a crisis response plan will actually work. To identify possible planning failures, decision makers can rely on independent outsiders to stress-test critical estimates in plans, to explore extreme scenarios, and to challenge optimistic assumptions about organizational performance during a crisis. This can lead to more realistic worst-case scenarios and the development of crisis response plans that are more robust. To avoid the pitfall of illusory redundancy, managers should carefully assess whether their backup plans are susceptible to the same risks as their regular operations. Rather than quickly narrowing their focus to the technical merits and challenges of a particular solution, executives should define the broad goals of the intended redundancy and identify counterexamples for which backup measures might also be vulnerable. The goal is for people to

shift their perspective and see redundancy as a vulnerable part of the system rather than as an invincible panacea.

These recommendations are not rocket science. They also don't require large financial investments or expensive technologies. That, however, does not mean that they are easy to implement. Indeed, getting organizations to heed dissenting voices, learn from small anomalies, and open themselves to independent scrutiny can be a difficult leadership challenge. And it's often extremely hard to change deeply ingrained routines for planning and decision making.

The good news is that these interventions don't necessarily clash with other key organizational priorities. Although it may seem that paying more attention to risk reduction, accident prevention, and safety will necessarily undermine a firm's focus on innovation and profits, the above-described solutions can actually enhance multiple organizational objectives. Team psychological safety, for example, is not only an effective safeguard against catastrophic risks but also a critical factor in the effectiveness and creativity of teams, as recent research at Google has revealed. Similarly, interventions that minimize the effect of cognitive biases in decision-making can not only reduce catastrophic risks but might also increase investment returns as well. Better management of catastrophic risks, it seems, can also lead to better management more generally.

About the author

 András Tilcsik, who is Hungarian-born, holds the Canada Research Chair in Strategy, Organizations, and Society at the Rotman School of Management and is a faculty fellow at the Michael Lee-Chin Family Institute for Corporate Citizenship. In 2015, he and Chris Clearfield won the Bracken Bower Prize from McKinsey and the *Financial Times*, given to the best business book proposal by scholars under 35. The book, *Meltdown: Why Our Systems Fail and What We Can Do About It* is forthcoming (Penguin, 2018). Tilcsik was shortlisted for the 2017 Thinkers50/Brightline Initiative Strategy Award.

A version of this article originally appeared as "Managing the Risk of Catastrophic Failure" in *Survive and Thrive: Winning Against Strategic Threats to Your Business* (edited by Joshua Gans and Sarah Kaplan), Dog Ear Publishing, 2017. Reprinted by permission.

'STRATEGIES ARE OKAYED IN BOARDROOMS THAT EVEN A CHILD WOULD SAY ARE BOUND TO FAIL. THE PROBLEM IS, THERE IS NEVER A CHILD IN THE BOARDROOM.'

VICTOR PALMIERI

ANIL GUPTA & HAIYAN WANG

The future of MNCs

The rising tide of economic nationalism has caused many observers to announce that globalization is not just in retreat, but near death. To be sure, the Brexit vote and the election of Donald Trump (as well as the popularity of various far-right European politicians) raise important questions about the future of free trade. But the future health of the multinational corporation is not in doubt. The outlook is good – but MNCs will need to adapt to some new realities.

First, let's put to rest the idea that globalization is on life support. By every important measure other than trade in goods, it's thriving. And the ongoing decline in merchandise trade long predates any changes in political sentiment.

It began soon after the global financial crisis of 2008. According to World Bank data, merchandise trade grew from 16 per cent of global GDP in 1990 to 26 per cent by 2008. Since then, it has been in steady decline and now stands at a little over 21 per cent of global GDP.

Political headwinds have almost nothing to do with the inability of merchandise trade to keep up with growth in world GDP. The actual culprits include the end of the commodities boom, rising costs in China, much slower growth in the major importing economies, ever-greater automation, and – as a result of the growing imperative for customer responsiveness – a push for shorter supply chains.

Many of these factors will become even more salient in the coming years. That fact – as well as the growing political clamor for local manufacturing – suggests that merchandise trade will be an even smaller driver of global integration in 2025 than it is today.

Casual observers routinely make the mistake of looking at global conomic integration almost solely through the lens of merchandise trade. In reality, though, economic integration is a multi-dimensional phenomenon encompassing merchandise trade, services trade, cross-border investments, and data flows. By every one of the latter three measures, global integration continues to thrive.

Trade in services has grown steadily from 4.0 per cent of world GDP in 1990 to 6.7 per cent today. Similarly, at 33.6 per cent of world GDP, global stock of FDI is higher today than it has ever been. And, according to McKinsey & Company, cross-border data flows today are more than 20 times what they were in 2005. In short, when looked at through that broader lens, global economic integration is alive and well. Its structure, however, is morphing. It was once led by trade; it's now led by investment. President Trump's call to Toyota to produce more within the U.S., rather than import more from elsewhere, is emblematic. Such calls will only gather steam.

The strategic implications for multinational corporations – be they Western, like GE and Siemens, or Asian, like Huawei and the Tata Group – are clear. They need to double down on localizing their operations in every major market. The design and specifications of products may remain largely standardized (think of MRI machines and smartphones) or may not (think of entertainment and food). Regardless, the actual production of goods and services will need to become more local.

Political leaders are almost always willing to let market forces dictate how global or local the design and features of products and services are. However, they do care whether a company brings investment and creates jobs. They care whether foreign companies become contributing citizens of their country, instead of operating as tourists.

An obvious caveat to the case for deeper localization is that the market must be large enough to enable efficient scale operations. While this is generally true of larger economies such as China, India, or Brazil, it may not be the case for, say, Saudi Arabia or Thailand. In the latter case, MNCs would be better off thinking in terms of regional localization.

Deeper localization can yield important additional benefits for MNCs. By reducing dependence on currency fluctuations, it should increase resilience. It should also enable the company to hire better local talent and strengthen its relationship with local governments. Both factors should enhance the company's competitiveness vis-à-vis local champions.

In his 2016 commencement speech at NYU, GE's CEO Jeff Immelt hit the nail on the head when he noted that the company's global future rests on a drive to deepen localization. This does not mean that GE needs to reinvent its digital strategy for every market. It does mean, however, that GE must invest and produce domestically more than it currently does within every major market. Every large company should be thinking along similar lines.

About the authors

Anil K. Gupta is the Michael D. Dingman Chair in Strategy, Globalization, and Entrepreneurship at the Smith School of Business, The University of Maryland.

Haiyan Wang is managing partner, China India Institute. They are the coauthors of *The Quest for Global Dominance*, *Getting China and India Right*, and *The Silk Road Rediscovered*.

'EACH OF US HAS SOMETHING OF VALUE TO OFFER – ALL 7.5 BILLION OF US. WHILE NOT EVERYONE WILL, ANYONE CAN. THE FACT THAT TODAY SO MANY PEOPLE DO NOT IS NOT A SIGN THAT THEY LACK CAPACITY, BUT INSTEAD IT'S A SIGN THAT THE SCAFFOLDING AND STRUCTURES NEED TO BE BUILT TO LET THEM DO SO. THIS IS SOCIETY'S PROBLEM, AND ITS OPPORTUNITY.'

NILOFER MERCHANT

SCOTT A. SNELL & KENNETH J. CARRIG

Beyond strategy: lessons of execution excellence

A couple of years ago, during a strategic review process at SunTrust, our analysis of the banking financial services industry revealed something very interesting: Strategy alone did not differentiate high- from low-performing firms. The true differentiator between winners and losers turned out to be how well the strategy was executed.

The data on this were fairly compelling, and it turns out the trend extends beyond banking. A Conference Board CEO Survey identified execution capability as the critical challenge facing today's business leaders. No one seems to disagree on the importance of execution, but a study by Bain & Company found that only about 15 per cent of companies truly have what we might call "high-performance organizations" (62 per cent are rated merely adequate, and a surprising 23 per cent actually have organizations that hold them back). Harvard Business School's John Kotter reinforced this concern, noting that 70 per cent of all strategic initiatives fail because of poor execution. Only 37 per cent of companies report that they are very good when it comes to execution (HBR survey, 2010).

Add it all up, and the conclusion seems to be glaringly obvious: (1) Execution is important both strategically and operationally, (2) many of us, regardless of industry sector, need to get better at it and (3) it is a leading cause for concern among CEOs.

Three lessons about execution

Over the past few years, we've been on a journey to focus on execution capability. And we've learned three important lessons along the way. First, although most everyone seems to agree that execution is critical, there is far less agreement on what is required to achieve it. Former Honeywell CEO Larry Bossidy noted in his book *Execution* that people believe they understand execution – "it's about getting things done" – but when asked how they get things done, "the dialogue goes rapidly downhill".

The second lesson we've learned is that moving from theory to practice can be just as challenging. One of our priorities for the project has been to identify a set of core metrics that allows us to assess a business unit's execution capability. To be candid, our goal has never been to zero in on every isolated element that affects performance. There's value in that approach, of course, but exhaustive measurement would likely lead to a cacophony of metrics that most CEOs would find unusable.

Third, we've learned that most metrics are primarily descriptive, much like a racecar's dashboard — they provide useful information, but in and of themselves they may not prevent accidents, maneuver around obstacles, or propel the car forward. We have adopted the metaphor of a navigation/guidance system that helps us make the right decisions, improves responsiveness, and accelerates growth and profitability. Over the past few years, we've been able to frame more clearly what execution excellence entails, but more importantly, we're learning what it requires.

The 4A Framework

So where do we start? At the end of the day, the performance of organizations depends on building an architecture that supports the collective abilities of individuals aligned toward achieving strategic outcomes. There are many important elements underlying execution excellence, but we focus on four: alignment, ability, architecture and agility.

The 4A model is not composed of four independent factors — they are integrally related, interdependent and mutually causal. Larry Bossidy and Ram Charan argued that "execution is a discipline," and we would not disagree. At the same time, we find it useful to think of execution capability more fundamentally as building the firm's resource base to energize performance. As shown in Figure 1, this is a system that combines human capital and organizational capital and that generates both potential and kinetic energy.

Ironically, we often refer to people and organizations as "resources," but less as sources of energy. In his work with senior executive teams, Jim Clawson emphasizes that "leadership is about managing energy, first in yourself and then in those around you." The same logic applies to strategy execution. Executives need to build the "ability" and "architecture" factors as sources of potential energy – the human potential and organizational potential that determine the firm's capacity to execute. At the same time, they need to foster "alignment" and "agility" as sources of kinetic energy — vitality that propels the firm into action. Alignment energizes performance by focusing and concentrating human resources. Agility energizes execution by channeling and accelerating it toward value-adding

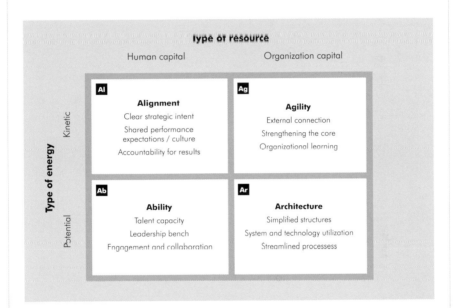

A4 Framework of execution capability

activities. Ask any leader with responsibility for strategy execution and he or she will tell you, "Resources are important; managing energy is essential."

Alignment: Focusing energy toward breakthrough performance

The *sine qua non* of execution capability is alignment. Organizations only exist because people can achieve more together than on their own. Alignment provides coherence, focus, energy and resilience in the face of change. And, not surprisingly, lack of alignment is a key source of divergent interests, conflict, dispersion and decay.

Three underlying elements in our model focus on the cognitive, affective and operational aspects of alignment:

Clear strategic intent. The clarity with which firms' strategy is devised, articulated, and communicated does make a difference. Two decades ago, Michael Treacy and Fred Wiersema described in their book, *The Discipline of Market Leaders*, that 75 per cent of the executive teams they studied could not clearly articulate their value proposition. The same can probably be said today, and, without a shared purpose, strategic intent and articulated strategy, it is difficult to establish a focal point for collective action and performance.

Shared performance expectations and culture. As the underlying foundation of the organization's culture, shared expectations serve both as points of aspired behavior and guardrails for acceptable action. But in the context of execution, shared expectations have to be operationalized as concrete behaviors driving performance, or else they get lost in the sea of good intentions and soft ideas.

Accountability for results. Many of those we work with assume that emphasis on accountability is a reaction to employee shirking. We think of the term more literally as "account" and "ability" combined. Without the ability to account for results toward a goal, it is difficult to create much focus for action or energize commitment toward it. Accountability requires establishing a set of performance metrics, feedback processes and shared outcomes (rewards) for performance.

Ability: Building human potential

People are an organization's greatest asset (there, we've promulgated the cliché). But the truth is that many organizations have faltered while burgeoning with talented people. And, if we were brutally honest, we'd admit that organizations traditionally have worked to take people out of the production equation in order to improve execution, preferring to substitute technologies for humans. But in the contemporary setting, where knowledge is a vital ingredient for both efficiency and effectiveness, that would be a mistake.

We focus on three aspects of an organization's human capital:

Talent capacity. Like any capital investment, the "make or buy" decisions for talent require tough choices about where payoffs will be greatest. Because HR budgets are often the first to be cut in difficult times, fewer dollars means more scrutinized investment. The priority with regard to execution is generating more high performers, particularly in critical roles.

Leadership bench. Leadership, beyond talent alone, often comes down to mobilizing excellence through others. Cultivating leaders requires longer lead times, of course, and therefore more enduring investment. As Wayne Gretzky, the great talent guru, said, "Skate to where the puck is going to be."

Engagement and collaboration. An organization's ability to execute ultimately depends on more than the skills of individuals or human capital. It extends to the social capital as well, the value of relationships and collaboration that drive collective achievement.

Architecture: Designing organizational capability

The design of organizations makes a big difference in terms of reliability, scalability and continuity of performance. So in terms of strategy execution, the organizational architecture is critical for managing resource flows, information availability, decision-making and process. We focus on three key aspects of the organization's architecture:

Simplified Structures. Although the adage "structure follows strategy" probably still applies, in terms of execution capability, the key is to simplify structures to eliminate needless complexity. The two fundamental purposes for structure are: (1) Delineate lines of authority and decision rights, and (2) improve channels of coordination and communication.

Information system access/utilization. It may come as no surprise that knowledge management is viewed by executives as the most important source of potential productivity gains over the next 15 years (Economist Intelligence Unit, 2006). The role of information technology affects execution capability in three principal ways: (1) operational, (2) relational and (3) transformational.

Streamlined processes. Technology investment without corresponding process redesign is like "paving cow paths." A whole cottage industry has arisen around the principles of process improvement and execution. At a minimum, execution is improved when processes and standard work are clearly defined, process owners are known and accountable, and measurement systems are used as a basis for decision-making.

Agility: Channeling value-added learning

There is an apocryphal story of Albert Einstein giving his assistant an exam to distribute to his graduate students. "But Professor Einstein," she said, "these are the same questions as last year." Einstein allegedly replied, "It's all right, the questions are the same, but the answers are different."

In high velocity environments, questions about growth, profitability, innovation, and the like may remain constant. But the answers may change rapidly. The key to execution increasingly depends on being agile, nimble, and proactive in the face of change and discontinuity. We focus on three requirements of agility for strategy execution, each of which provides a more proximal indicator of firm performance:

Customer and stakeholder connectivity. The importance of customer engagement might be overlooked if we assume that execution is a strictly internally focused capability. One of the worst things a company can do is to give into "chin down" management. In an effort to get the most from themselves and their people, too many managers will erroneously concentrate on the work in front of them and miss what is around them.

The primary attention needs to remain on the customer, but also attend to other relevant stakeholders in the environment. Where are the faint signals that could define the future? The engagement needs to be active, not passive; probing the environment to see how it responds.

Innovation and organization learning. Agile companies approach execution in terms rapid response, small experiments, rapid testing and learning, and flexible resource allocation. These need not be 'bet the company' investments, but perhaps are small experiments to learn. The more of these experiments, the more the organization begins to resemble an ecosystem of possible futures. And more variety in the ecosystem increases the likelihood of survival. Experts in the field of innovation make a distinction between two types of organizational learning: (1) exploration, which is going into new domains, and (2) exploitation, which is deeper learning within the current domain. Without developing deeper expertise in current product/service domains, a firm's execution capability will stall.

Strengthen the core. Any athlete will tell you that agility requires core strength. The core of an organization, obviously, is the central capabilities for value creation. Ironically, one might presume that agility would benefit from flexibility and not investing too much in one area. Just the opposite is true; organizations that invest consistently in the core knowledge have a basis of strength to respond to the market Conversely, an organization with a weak core has a difficult time pivoting to anything (opportunities or threats).

About the authors

Scott A Snell holds the E Thayer Bigelow Research Chair and is the former Senior Associate Dean for Executive Education at the University of Virginia's Darden School of Business.

Kenneth J Carrig is Chief Human Resources Officer at SunTrust.

This is an adapted version of their paper "In Search of Execution," included in *View From the Top: Leveraging Human Capital to Create Value* (Society for Human Resource Management).

Resources

Bossidy, Larry & Charan, Ram, Execution, Crown Business, 2002.

Clawson, James G, Level Three Leadership (third edition), Prentice Hall, 2005.

Treacy, Michael and Wiersema, Fred, *The Discipline of Market Leaders*, Basic Books, 1995.